S0-AKD-082

CONTENTS

EXERCISES FOR

English Simplified

Eighth Edition

Blanch Ellsworth
John A. Higgins
Revised by Judith Olson-Fallon
Case Western Reserve University

LONGMAN

Longman is an imprint of Addison Wesley Longman

Exercises **for**
Ellsworth/Higgins *English Simplified*
Eighth Edition

Copyright © 1997 Longman Publishers USA, a division of Addison Wesley Longman, Inc.

ISBN: 0-673-97630-0

97 98 99 00 01 9 8 7 6 5 4 3 2

PREFACE

The eighth edition of *Exercises for English Simplified* continues to offer a wide range of English exercises for a variety of academic settings. Studying *English Simplified* and working through the exercises can be a student's first step in establishing an effective proofreading process for writing. By completing the appropriate exercises, students can isolate and understand the nature of their proofreading problems. By working in peer editing groups, students can then transfer what they learned from *English Simplified* to their writing.

Special features of *Exercises for English Simplified* include the following:

1. Exercises for all major topics discussed in the seventh edition of *English Simplified* including proofreading MLA and APA citations
2. Diagnostic and achievement tests to assess students' initial performance and later progress
3. Examples and sentences reflecting both contemporary issues and the concerns of a diverse student population
4. Exercises requiring students to provide not only the correct answer but also the reasons for their choices
5. A brief glossary, a list of grammatical terms, and an index to *English Simplified* for quick and easy cross-referencing

Longman Publishers wishes to acknowledge the expert advice offered by the following reviewers during the revision of *Exercises for English Simplified:* Robert Dees, Orange Coast College; H. Brown Miller, City College of San Francisco; Joseph A. Scherer, Community College of Allegheny; Cam Tinnell, Longwood College; Betty Jeane Wallace, Sinclair Community College; and Ted McFerrin, Collin County Community College.

1. DIAGNOSTIC TEST: GRAMMAR

Sentences

In the blank after each item,

Write **1** if the boldface expression is **one complete sentence.**
Write **2** if it is a **fragment** (incorrect: less than a complete sentence).
Write **3** if it is a **comma splice** or a **fused sentence** (incorrect: two or more sentences written as one; also known as a **run-on**).

Example: Thoreau spent the night in jail. **Having refused to pay his taxes.**   _____2_____

1. The choir had brought their music. **However, no one asked them to sing.**   1._____

2. The President eventually seemed happy to retire from politics. **His family looking forward to spending more time with him.**   2._____

3. **In Russia, pork is sold for 465 rubles a pound that amount is equivalent to the average monthly salary.**   3._____

4. The Yankees made two big trades after the season had begun. **First for a shortstop and then for a center fielder.**   4._____

5. The African American Society put Martina Jones in charge of the Multicultural Festival. **A responsibility that appealed to her.**   5._____

6. **The boys are learning traditional Irish dancing, they really seem to enjoy their dance class.**   6._____

7. Divorce is still prevalent in America. **Four out of every thousand people.**   7._____

8. **Although American society may seem uncaring, more people are volunteering to help with the homeless.**   8._____

9. **The reason for her shyness being that she knew no one at the party except her hostess.**   9._____

10. **The experiment to produce nuclear fusion was both controversial and exciting, scientists all over the world attempted to duplicate its results.**   10._____

11. **Scientists have learned that bison can infect livestock with a serious bacterial disease.**   11._____

12. She loved all styles of art. **She said she particularly loved the impressionists, she had studied them in Paris.**   12._____

13. We walked over to the lost-and-found office. **To see whether the bag had been turned in.**   13._____

14. **The shift lever must be in neutral only then will the car start.**   14._____

15. **The weather has been so harsh this winter, it's snowed almost every day.** Everyone is sick of shoveling snow.   15._____

16. **If you want an unusual form of exercise, learn to play the bagpipes.**   16._____

Grammar

Write **1** if the boldface expression is used **correctly**.
Write **2** if it is used **incorrectly**.

Example: There **is** just three shopping days before Christmas.   ___2___

1. The professor assured Mark and **I** that we could still pass the course.   1. _____

2. Bill was fired from his new job, **which** made him despondent.   2. _____

3. Each member will be responsible for **their** own transportation.   3. _____

4. There **was** at least five computers in the office.   4. _____

5. Several of **us** newcomers needed a map to find our way around.   5. _____

6. Every adminstrator and faculty member **was** required to attend the orientation
    program.   6. _____

7. The graduate teaching assistant and **myself** met for a review session.   7. _____

8. Surprisingly enough, presidential candidate Joan Smith was leading **not only** in
    the cities **but also** in the rural areas.   8. _____

9. In each sack lunch **were** a cheese sandwich, an apple, and a soda.   9. _____

10. Leave the message with **whoever** answers the phone.   10. _____

11. **Having made no other plans for the evening,** Tony was glad to accept
    the invitation.   11. _____

12. Everyone in the Hispanic Society **was** urged to join the movement to bring
    more Hispanic faculty to campus.   12. _____

13. If I **were** driving to Pennsylvania this weekend, I would take along my sketch pad. 13. _____

14. I bought one of the printers that **were** on sale.   14. _____

15. There **were** five different Asian student organizations on campus.   15. _____

16. **Do** either of you know the source of that quotation?   16. _____

17. The director, as well as the choir members, **has** agreed to appear on television. 17. _____

18. The supervisor is especially fond of arranging training programs, working on
    elaborate projects, and to **develop budgets.**   18. _____

19. Zack, **hoping to impress Tomiko with his knowledge of Japanese cooking,**
    is preparing an elaborate meal.   19. _____

20. **Who** do you think mailed the anonymous letter to the editor?   20. _____

21. Neither the students nor the instructor **knows** where the notice is to be posted. 21. _____

22. Are you sure that it was **him** that you saw last evening?   22. _____

23. Between you and **me**, her decision to transfer to another department was not
    well received by her current supervisor.   23. _____

24. Hoping to find part-time employment, Anthony **made** an appointment at the
    campus placement office.   24. _____

25. He joined the Big Brothers Organization and coached in Little League. **It** was
    expected of him by his law firm.   25. _____

26. Given the candidates, it's painfully clear that **us** voters didn't have much of a choice. 26 _____

27. Customers should check the fruit carefully before paying; otherwise, **you** may end up with rotten or spoiled fruit.

27. _____

28. Anyone who forgets his book will not be able to take **their** report home

28. _____

29. While carrying my books to the library, **a squirrel darted across my path.**

29. _____

30. Norma **only** had one issue left to raise before she could rest her case.

30. _____

31. I had no idea that **my** giving a report would create such turmoil at the meeting.

31. _____

32. We didn't think that many of **us** substitutes would get into the game.

32. _____

33. Dean Robert Patterson gave Karen and **I** permission to establish a volunteer organization to tutor students from city schools.

33. _____

34. Although he often spoke harshly to others, his voice sounded **pleasant** to us.

34. _____

35. Neither the librarian nor the students in the reference room **was** aware of the situation.

35. _____

36. Professor Rogers looks very **differently** since he dyed his beard and moustache.

36. _____

37. There is no question that it was **she** under the table.

37. _____

38. Bob had always been more curious about the family's French ancestors than **he.**

38. _____

39. Dr. Smith, together with thirty of his students, **are** working at a community service site.

39. _____

40. Each of the e**were** given a set of business cards.

40. _____

41. Fast motorcyles **are** his passion.

41. _____

42. **Standing motionless on the windswept, dreary plain,** the rain pelted my face.

42. _____

43. I had agreed to **promptly and without delay** notify them of my decision.

43. _____

44. The dean agreed to award the scholarship to **whomever** the committee selected.

44. _____

45. **Knowing that I should study,** it seemed important to unplug the phone.

45. _____

46. **Who** were you looking for in the auditorium?

46. _____

47. The noise and the general chaos caused by the alarm **were** disturbing to the visitor.

47. _____

48. As hard as I try, I'll never be as thin as **her.**

48. _____

49. Only one of these stamps **is** of real value.

49. _____

50. The guide showed Carol and **myself** the bus routes.

50. _____

2. DIAGNOSTIC TEST: PUNCTUATION

In the blank after each sentence,

Write **1** if the punctuation in brackets is **correct**;
Write **0** if it is **incorrect**.

(Use only one number in each blank.)

Example: Regular exercise and sound nutritional habits[,] are essential for good health.   ___0___

Example: Mr[.] Elliot worked in a bank   ___1___

1. Modern writers are often influenced by the past[;] in fact, we can't fully study their work without knowing the traditions they draw on.   1._____

2. A good horror movie doesn't merely scare us[,] it shows us worlds we never imagined.   2._____

3. "Why can't a woman be more like a man["?] the chauvinist asked.   3._____

4. I learned that the newly elected officers were Marzell Brown, president[;] Leroy Jones, vice president[;] Sandra Smith, treasurer[;] and James Chang, secretary.   4._____

5. The class expected low grades[. T]he test having been long and difficult.   5._____

6. It[']s hard to imagine life without a VCR, a personal computer, and a microwave oven.   6._____

7. Eventually, everybody comes to Rick's[;] the best saloon in Casablanca.   7._____

8. Recognizing that busing places stress on younger students[,] the state officials are restructuring its transportation system.   8._____

9. Richard Hernandez was unhappy at his college[,] he missed hearing Spanish and enjoying his favorite foods.   9._____

10. That is not the Sullivans' boat; at least, I think that it isn't their[']s.   10._____

11. When it rains, I always think of the opening lines of Longfellow's poem "The Rainy Day": "The day is cold, and dark, and dreary [/] It rains, and the wind is never weary."   11._____

12. Inspector Trace asked, "Is that all you remember?[" "]Are you sure?"   12._____

13. "The report is ready," Chisholm said[,] "I'm sending it to the supervisor today."   13._____

14. Didn't I hear you say, "I especially like blueberry pie"[?]   14._____

15. Joe enrolled in a small college[;] although he had planned originally to join a rock band.   15._____

16. Stanley moved to Minneapolis[,] where he hoped to open a restaurant.   16._____

17. That was a bit too close for comfort[,] wasn't it?   17._____

18. The advertiser received more than two[-]hundred replies on the Internet.   18._____

19. Sarah is asking for a week[']s vacation to visit relatives in Canada.   19._____

20. On February 21, 1997[,] Robin and Sam are getting married.   20._____

21. The womens['] basketball team has reached the state finals. 21. _____

22. Recently, researchers have discovered that rhesus monkeys have some hidden talents[;] such as the ability to do basic math. 22. _____

23. She received twenty[-]three greeting cards on her sixtieth birthday. 23. _____

24. He caught the pass[,] and dashed for the end zone. 24. _____

25. Many weeks before school was out[;] he had applied for a summer job. 25. _____

26. Dear Sir[;] Please accept this letter of application for the teaching position. 26. _____

27. Schweitzer summed up his ethics as "reverence for life[,]" a phrase that came to him during his early years in Africa. 27. _____

28. Our communications professor asked us if we understood the use of extended periods of silence often found in conversations among Native Americans[?] 28. _____

29. "As for who won the election[—]well, not all the votes have been counted," she said. 29. _____

30. [']The Perils of Aerobic Dancing['] (This is the title of a student's composition for an English class.) 30. _____

31. Any music[,] that is not jazz[,] does not appeal to him. 31. _____

32. "Election results are coming in quickly now," the newscaster announced[;] "and we should be able to predict the winner soon." 32. _____

33. Over forty-two percent of all adults over eighteen are single[,] however, over ninety percent of these adults will marry at least once. 33. _____

34. The children went to the zoo[;] bought ice-cream cones[;] fed peanuts to the elephants[;] and watched the seals perform their tricks while being fed. 34. _____

35. [']For He's a Jolly Good Fellow['] is my grandfather's favorite song to sing at birthday parties. 35. _____

36. In the early 1900s, department stores provided customers electric lighting, public telephones, and escalators[;] and these stores offered countless other services, such as post offices, branch libraries, root gardens and in-store radio stations. 36. _____

37. Watch out[,] Marlene, for icy patches on the sidewalk. 37. _____

38. Late-night television viewers should be cautious when watching a home-shopping network[,] because they may purchase items that they don't need. 38. _____

39. Because he stayed up to play computer games[,] he didn't make it to his early class. 39. _____

40. The weather[—]rain, rain, and more rain[—]has ruined our weekend plans for an entire month. 40. _____

41. The first modern drive-in was called[,] The Pig Stand, which was a barbecue pit along a highway between Dallas and Fort Worth. 41. _____

42. The scholarship award went to Julia Brown, the student[,] who had the highest grades. 42. _____

43. Some of the technologies developed after World War II were[:] television, synthetic fibers, and air travel. 43. _____

44. The Lincoln Highway[,] which was the first transcontinental highway[,] officially opened in 1923 and was advertised as America's Main Street. 44. _____

45. Esther Greenberg[,] who is my roommate[,] comes from a small town. 45. _____

46. I hav[']ent made up my mind whether I want a computer system with an attached video camera. 46. _____

47. The talk show host[,] irritated and impatient[,] cut off the caller who insisted he was calling from aboard a flying saucer.

47. _____

48. Author Mike Rose writes[:] "When a local public school is lost to incompetence, indifference, or despair, it should be an occasion for mourning. . . ."

48. _____

49. A note under the door read: "Sorry you weren't in. The Emerson[']s."

49. _____

50. Most of my friends are upgrading their computer systems[,] they want to use CD ROM software at home.

50. _____

51. This spring we began a new family vacation tradition[:] we flew to Florida to watch the Indians' spring training.

51. _____

52. No matter how cute they look, squirrels[,] in my opinion[,] are very destructive rodents.

52. _____

53. We are planning a trip to Chicago[,] the children will enjoy the city's museums.

53. _____

54. By saving her money[,] Laura was able to build her cottage on the lake.

54. _____

55. To gain recognition as a speaker[;] he accepted all invitations to appear before civic groups.

55. _____

56. Charles Wright[,] who survived an avalanche in the Himalayas[,] thought he heard a flute right before the storm occurred.

56. _____

57. Any candidate[,] who wants to increase social spending[,] will probably be defeated during the upcoming elections.

57. _____

58. "Oh dear[,] I hope I'm not late," said Irma.

58. _____

59. "I cannot believe that you have not read my book!"[,] shouted the author to the critic.

59. _____

60. In his painting *The Red Dog,* the French artist Paul Gauguin painted people from Tahiti in a bold and bright style.

60. _____

61. While there are many ideas about how the bullpen in baseball got its name[,] many writers think its because Bull Durham tobacco ads were often posted near the area where pitchers practiced between innings.

61. _____

62. According to my family's written records, my great-grandfather was born in 1870[,] and died in 1895.

62. _____

63. My hometown is a place[,] where older men still think white shoes and belts are high fashion.

63. _____

64. She spent her student teaching practicum in Johnstown(,) where she went to hockey games each week.

64. _____

65. Having learned that she was eligible for a scholarship[,] she turned in her application.

65. _____

66. Living in his car for three weeks[,] did not especially bother him.

66. _____

67. Stand with your hips flush against the wall[,] then see how far forward you can bend without losing your balance.

67. _____

68. Many Americans remember family celebrations from their childhood[,] moreover, they are seeking ways to incorporate some of these rituals into their busy lives.

68. _____

69. In 1888, a bank clerk named George Eastman created the first amateur camera called the Detective Camera[;] this camera was a small black box with a button and a key for advancing the film.

69. _____

70. After the long, harsh winter, I needed a soak in[-]the[-]sun vacation.

70. _____

71. The real estate agent[,] who sold our house[,] offered many tips on how to prepare our house for the market.

71. _____

72. Never leave the car unattended in the parking lot[!]   72. _____

73. The parking lot always is full[,] when there is a concert.   73. _____

74. Dan was proud that he received all A[']s.   74. _____

75. The student promised to finish the paper[,] and turn it in by the end of the day.   75. _____

3. DIAGNOSTIC TEST: MECHANICS, SPELLING, USAGE

Capitalization

In each blank, write **1** if the boldface word(s) **follow** the rules of capitalization;

write **0** if they do not.

Example: Edgar Allan Poe was born in **Boston**. __1__

Example: She comes from my **City**. __0__

1. I read a book about the *Titanic*. 1.____
2. My **college** days were stressful. 2.____
3. He attends Taft **high school**. 3.____
4. The **President** vetoed the bill. 4.____
5. We planned to vacation in the **East**. 5.____
6. We presented **Mother** with a bouquet of roses. 6.____
7. I finally passed **spanish**. 7.____
8. She is in France; **He** is at home. 8.____
9. "Are you working?" **she** asked. 9.____
10. I love **Korean** food. 10.____

11. We saluted the **american** flag. 11.____
12. Last **Summer** I drove to California. 12.____
13. My birthday was on **Friday**. 13.____
14. I am enrolled in courses in **philosophy** and Japanese. 14.____
15. She went **North** for Christmas. 15.____
16. Please, **Father**, lend me your car. 16.____
17. My **Aunt** Harriet wrote a novel. 17.____
18. "Stop!" **shouted** the officer. 18.____
19. Jane refused to be **Chairperson** of the committee. 19.____
20. "If possible," he said, "**Write** the report today. 20.____

Abbreviations and Numbers

Write **1** if the boldface abbreviation or number is used **correctly**;
Write **0** it is used **incorrectly.**

Example: I love **NY**. __0__

1. **Three million** people have visited the park. 1.____
2. I participated in a **five-hour** workshop on interpersonal communications. 2.____
3. The play begins at **7 p.m.** 3.____
4. Aaron was born on November **11th,** 1988. 4.____
5. The rent is **$325** a month. 5.____
6. The interest comes to **8** percent. 6.____
7. I need the background information, the statistics, **and etc.** 7.____

8. There are **nineteen** women in the club. 8.____
9. **1995** was another bad year for flooding. 9.____
10. I wrote a note to **Dr.** Levy. 10.____
11. He works at the Swiss Import **Co.** 11.____
12. She lives on Buchanan **Ave.** 12.____
13. We consulted Ricardo Guitierrez, **Ph.D.** 13.____
14. Our appointment is at **4** o'clock. 14.____
15. I slept only **3** hours last night. 15.____

Spelling

In each sentence, one boldface word is **misspelled**; write its number in the blank.

Example: (1)**Its**(2)**too** late (3)**to** go.   __1__

1. Jane's (1)**independent** attitude sometimes was a (2)**hindrence** to the (3)**committee**.   1._____

2. (1)**Approximatly** half of the class noticed the (2)**omission** of the last item on the (3)**questionnaire**.   2._____

3. The (1)**mischievous** child was (2)**usualy** (3)**courteous** to adults.   3._____

4. At the office, Jack was described as an (1)**unusually** (2)**conscientous** and (3)**indispensable** staff member.   4._____

5. Even though Dave was (1)**competent** in his (2)**mathematics** class, he didn't have the (3)**disipline** required to work through the daily homework.   5._____

6. The sociologist's (1)**analysis** of the (2)**apparent** (3)**prejudise** that existed among the villagers was insightful.   6._____

7. She was (1)**particularly** (2)**sensable** about maintaining a study (3)**schedule**.   7._____

8. It was (1)**necesary** to curb Tad's (2)**tendency** to interrupt the staff discussion with (3)**irrelevant** comments.   8._____

9. (1)**Personaly**, it was no (2)**surprise** that (3)**curiosity** prompted the toddler to smear lipstick on the bathroom mirror.   9._____

10. Tim developed a (1)**procedure** for updating our (2)**bussiness** (3)**calendar**.   10._____

11. As a (1)**sophomore**, Sue had the (2)**perseverence** and (3)**sacrifice** needed to work three part-time jobs and to raise her three sons.   11._____

12. Her (1)**opinion**, while (2)**fascinating**, revealed an indisputable (3)**hypocricy**.   12._____

13. Every day our (1)**secretery** meets a colleague from the (2)**Psychology** Department at their favorite campus (3)**restaurant**.   13._____

14. During (1)**adolescence** we often (2)**condemm** anyone who offers (3)**guidance**.   14._____

15. Based on Bill's (1)**description**, his dream vacation sounded (2)**irrestable** and guaranteed to (3)**fulfill** anyone's need to escape.   15._____

Usage

Write **1** if the boldface expression is used **correctly**;
write **0** if it is used **incorrectly**.

Example: Sacramento is the state **capitol**.   __0__

1. Her car is different **than** mine.   1.____

2. I'm not sick; I'm **alright**.   2.____

3. The plane began its **descent** for Denver.   3.____

4. Economic problems always **impact** our enrollment.   4.____

5. My glasses **lay** where I had put them.   5.____

6. I **seldom ever** exercise in the morning.   6.____

7. We didn't play **good** in the last quarter.   7.____

8. I selected a **nice** birthday card.   8.____

9. The float **preceded** the band in the parade. 9.____

10. No one predicted the **affects** of the bomb. 10.____

11. My aunt always uses unusual **stationery**. 11.____

12. I dislike **those kind** of cookies. 12.____

13. We are going to **canvas** the school district for the scholarship fund. 13.____

14. The computer **sits** on a small table. 14.____

15. The mayor was pleased to announce that a **woman firefighter** was promoted to captain. 15.____

16. The **principal** spoke to the students. 16.____

17. I **had ought** to learn to use that software. 17.____

18. **On the basis of** the report, the committee hired a consultant. 18.____

19. **Almost** everyone had left. 19.____

20. He made **less** mistakes than I did. 20.____

21. The family **better** repair the furnace. 21.____

22. The package had **burst** open. 22.____

23. Mrs. Grundy **censured** so much of the play that it was unintelligible. 23.____

24. We are taught to consider the feelings of our **fellow man**. 24.____

25. **Irregardless** of the warning, I drove in the dense fog. 25.____

26. The chairperson said only one meaningful **thing** at the meeting. 26.____

27. The new carpet **complements** the living room furniture. 27.____

28. An **individual** will have to chair the service project. 28.____

29. I phoned **in regard to** employment. 29.____

30. I **ought to of** made the flight arrangements. 30.____

4. GRAMMAR: PARTS OF A SENTENCE

(Study 1-3, The The Sentence and Its Parts)

Select the number which marks the point where the **complete subject** ends and the **complete predicate** begins.

Example: Recently(1) the United States(2) has suffered several(3) severe weather disasters.   ___2___

1. The Statue of Liberty (1) was restored (2) and reopened (3) in 1988.   1._____

2. Many of the abandoned railroad stations (1) of America and Canada (2) have been restored (3) for other uses.   2._____

3. Artist Henri (1) Matisse, who lived to be eighty-four years old, (2) left a legacy of paintings, paper cutouts, sculptures, drawings (3) and prints.   3._____

4. The editor (1) wrote a kind note (2) after the long list of changes(3) to be made before final printing.   4._____

5. Word processors, (1) with their power to make editing easy, (2) allow writers to revise (3) as often as they wish.   5._____

6. I (1) recently completed (2) a twenty-page research paper (3) on the proposed common currency for all European countries.   6._____

7. Which (1) of the three word-processing software packages (2) has (3) the best thesaurus?   7._____

8. Rarely would she drive her car after the earthquakes.

    [This inverted-word-order sentence, rewritten in subject-predicate order, becomes: She (1) would rarely (2) drive (3) her car (4) after the earthquakes.]   8._____

9. Which (1) of the polls (2) examined the impact (3) of the decline of an economic base in urban areas?   9._____

10. When did the committee select the candidate to hire? [Rewritten in subject-predicate order: The committee (1) did select (2) the candidate (3) to hire when?]   10._____

Write **1** if the boldface word is a **subject** (or part of a compound subject).
Write **2** if it is a **predicate** (verb).
Write **3** if it is a **complement** (or part of a compound complement).

Example: Wendell played a great game.   ___1___

Example: Wendell played a great **game.**   ___3___

Example: The **crew** of the ship was afraid.   ___1___

Example: The crew of the ship **was** afraid.   ___2___

1. **All** perform their tragic play.   1._____

2.   All perform their tragic **play**.   2. _____

3.   Champion athletes **spend** much time training and competing.   3. _____

4.   Champion athletes spend much **time** training and competing.   4. _____

5.   **Sue** and Janet enjoy gardening.   5. _____

6.   Sue and **Janet** enjoy gardening.   6. _____

7.   Many **athletes** worry about life after the pros.   7. _____

8.   Many athletes **worry** about life after the pros.   8. _____

9.   The **populist theme** from the last election may survive until the next election.   9. _____

10. The populist theme from the last election **may survive** until the next election.   10. _____

11. The **neighborhood** worked hard to clean up the local playground.   11. _____

12. The neighborhood **worked** hard to clean up the local playground.   12. _____

13. The clustered **lights** far below the plane were cities.   13. _____

14. The clustered lights far below the plane were **cities**.   14. _____

15. A beacon **lights** the runway for arriving planes at night.   15. _____

16. A beacon lights the **runway** for arriving planes at night.   16. _____

17. Often the consequences of being fired in a career are personal **depression** and
     economic hardship.   17. _____

18. Often the consequences of being fired in a career are personal depression and
     economic **hardship**.   18. _____

19. **We** peeked at the latest draft of Sam's romance novel.   19. _____

20. We **peeked** at the latest draft of Sam's romance novel.   20. _____

5. GRAMMAR: PARTS OF SPEECH

(Study 4-9, The Parts of Speech: A Survey)

Write the number (**1** to **8** from the list below) of the **part of speech** of each boldface word.

1. noun	**3. verb**	**5. adverb**	**7. conjunction**
2. pronoun	**4. adjective**	**6. preposition**	**8. interjection**

Example: Hawthorne wrote **stories**. ___1___

1. Molly is a **singer** in a band. 1.____
2. You must **replace** the alternator. 2.____
3. **She** anticipated the vote. 3.____
4. The new law affected **all**. 4.____
5. Robert felt **tired**. 5.
6. She was **here** a moment ago. 6.____
7. The **primary** goal is to reduce spending. 7.____
8. The test was hard **but** fair. 8.____
9. Do you want fries **with** that? 9.____
10. **This** book is mine. 10.____
11. **This** is the car to buy. 11.____
12. She lives **across** the street. 12.____
13. Is this **your** book? 13.____
14. The book is **mine**. 14.____
15. He wants an **education**. 15.____
16. **Oh dear,** the professor looks confused. 16.____
17. He agreed to proceed **slowly**. 17.____
18. They **were sleeping** soundly at noon. 18.____
19. The candidate selected a **charismatic** running mate. 19.____
20. She is **unusually** talented. 20.____
21. **Everyone** joined in the protest. 21.____
22. The **synagogue** is a landmark. 22.____
23. Students from all over the state **had** come to the rally. 23.____
24. The workers took a **strike** vote. 24.____

25. He is the one **whom** I suspect. 25.____
26. The researcher played a video game **while** waiting for the results. 26.____
27. What is your **plan**? 27.____
28. Nancy **is** a feminist. 28.____
29. No one came **after** ten o'clock. 29.____
30. Put the book **there**. 30.____
31. I saw him **once**. 31.____
32. The **theater** was dark. 32.____
33. The tribe owns a **factory**. 33.____
34. Weren't **you** surprised? 34.____
35. They waited **for** us. 35.____
36. The oil spill was very **damaging**. 36.____
37. Did you pay your **dues**? 37.____
38. **All** survivors were calm. 38.____
39. **All** were calm. 39.____
40. The student read **quickly**. 40.____
41. She **became** an executive. 41.____
42. **Well**, what shall we do now? 42.____
43. He worked **during** the summer. 43.____
44. **Tomorrow** is her birthday. 44.____
45. Will she call **tomorrow**? 45.____
46. **If** I go, will you come? 46.____
47. The executive stood **behind** her staff. 47.____
48. He should never **have been advanced** in rank. 48.____
49. The **wild** party was finally over. 49.____
50. Iris arrived at the park **early**. 50.____

6. GRAMMAR: PARTS OF SPEECH

Study 4-9, The Parts of Speech: A Survey)

Write the number (**1** to **8** from the list below) of the **part of speech** of each boldface word.

1. noun	3. verb	5. adverb	7. conjunction
2. pronoun	4. adjective	6. preposition	8. interjection

Example: **Emilio** planned to become a surgeon. _1_

1. **Clarify** what you mean. 1.____
2. The letter should arrive **today**. 2.____
3. **What** is the theme of the poem? 3.____
4. She **never** confides in anyone. 4.____
5. **May** I **call** you early on Friday? 5.____
6. **Scary** monsters crept into the little boy's dreams. 6.____
7. The weather was gray **and** miserable. 7.____
8. They **are** both on the football team. 8.____
9. **Which** is your locker? 9.____
10. Write to me **when** you can. 10.____
11. **He** cannot believe her reply. 11.____
12. **Neither** of the candidates spoke. 12.____
13. **The** vacation proved quite hazardous. 13.___
14. The **house** was quiet. 14.____
15. With a few more votes, Hansen **would have been elected**. 15.____
16. **Ah**, I thought you would agree. 16.____
17. She spoke with genuine **feeling**. 17.____
18. Mr. Wilson **is** a registered pharmacist. 18.____
19. The jury decided that there was **criminal** intent. 19.____
20. The students **are calculating** their grade point averages. 20.____
21. **Maple** trees in Vermont are threatened by acid rain. 21.____

22. He objected **strenuously**. 22.____
23. This plane goes **to** Cleveland. 23.____
24. He is a real **diplomat**. 24.____
25. **Unless** you qualify, you will be unable to compete. 25.____
26. Rosa stood **motionless**. 26.____
27. Henry **eagerly** drove to the office because he remembered that his boss was out of town. 27.____
28. Give the report to either Jack **or** Emily. 28.____
29. The new television shows were predictable **and** disappointing. 29.____
30. Do you recognize **this** name? 30.____
31. **Somebody** will surely notify you. 31.____
32. She lives **on** a ranch in Idaho. 32.____
33. The motive for the crime will **soon** become clear. 33.____
34. **This** is a thankless task. 34.____
35. Please **accept** her offer without delay. 35.____
36. I arrived **too** late to see him. 36.____
37. Everybody talks **about** the weather. 37.____
38. The senator spoke **cautiously** about increasing taxes. 38.____
39. You are **now** approaching Paris. 39.____
40. The car was not new, but **it** was in good condition. 40.____
41. **Roth** never published a second novel. 41.____

42. He **has** always **liked** good food. 42.____

43. We plan to make **an** early start. 43.____

44. I want an **up-to-date** directory. 44.____

45. The animosity **between** the representatives was ardent. 45.____

46. The country **should have established** better trade agreements with the major industrial powers. 46.____

47. He fell **because** he was dizzy. 47.____

48. **None** of the students failed. 48.____

49. Van began to play **beautifully**. 49.____

50. Supplies were **not** available. 50.____

Name _____ Class _____ Date _____ Score (R_____ x 2)_____

7. GRAMMAR: PARTS OF SPEECH AND THEIR USES

(Study 4-9, The Parts of Speech: A Survey)

First, write the number (**1** to **8**, from the list below) of the **part of speech** of each boldface word. Then, write the number (**9** to **25**, from the list below) that tells how the word is used.

1. noun
2. pronoun

9. subject
10. direct object
11. indirect object
12. subjective complement
13. objective complement
14. object of preposition

3. verb   15. predicate

4. adjective

16. modifying noun or pronoun
17. subjective complement
18. objective complement

5. adverb

19. modifying verb
20. modifying adjective
21. modifying adverb

6. preposition   22. introducing prepositional phrase

7. conjunction

23. coordinating:joining words, phrases, or clauses of equal rank
24. subordinating:introducing dependent clause

8. interjection   25. showing emotion

	Part of Speech	Use
Example: The **Giants** were defeated.	1	9

1. You **expect** me to believe that?   1.____ ____

2. The judges declared Julie the winner.   2.____ ____

3. **What!** It can't be true!   3.____ ____

4. A **spreading** pessimism hit the stock market.   4.____ ____

5. Donate **them** to the homeless.   5.____ ____

6. He seems **unfriendly.**   6.____ ____

7. Debbie gave the book to **me.**   7.____ ____

8. We'll have our picnic **after** the game.   8.____ ____

9. Sam called me **lazy.**   9.____ ____

10. Jane will be the **principal** for our neighborhood elementary school.   10.____ ____

11. Denny paved the **driveway.**   11.____ ____

12. I must work hard, **for** I have several major scholarships.   12.____ ____

13. Troy gave **me** the book.   13.____ ____

14. She spoke **very** slowly.   14.____ ____

15. The **repetition** gets boring after a while.   15.____ ____

16. The prize was a **night** on the town.   16.____ ____

17. He drives **carefully.**   17.____ ____

18. **Before** we took the exam, our professor gave a brief review.   18.____ ____

19. Many Vietnam vets cry **at** the monument.   19.____ ____

20. Most city officials consider the mayor an expert **negotiator.**   20.____ ____

21. We rented a **camper.**   21.____ ____

22. **Because** it's late, let's order out
    for supper.   22.____ ____

23. The path was **muddy.**   23.____ ____

24. She looked **good** in her new
    professional attire.   24.____ ____

25. I was **too** surprised to answer.   25.____ ____

26. Repeat the first **step.**   26.____ ____

27. **Who** will be first to speak?   27.____ ____

28. The coach made Joseph the
    catcher.   28.____ ____

29. He played **very** well.   29.____ ____

30. **Since** the weather is unpredictable,
    we'll stage the debate inside.   30.____ ____

31. **Watch** for falling rocks!   31.____ ____

32. The governor gave **Thompson**
    an order.   32.____ ____

33. He ran **quickly.**   33.____ ____

34. **"Hurrah!"** we yelled.   34.____ ____

35. The emergency crew seemed
    very **slow.**   35.____ ____

36. Has he **called?**   36.____ ____

37. The American sports culture is
    complex.   37.____ ____

38. I wrote a summary at the end
    of my **paper.**   38.____ ____

39. My son gave his **friend** a poster. 39.____ ____

40. **Everyone** enjoyed the
    presentation.   40.____ ____

41. He seems **truly** sorry.   41.____ ____

42. **Oh my,** I have misplaced my car
    keys again.   42.____ ____

43. Jack had an **odd** look on his face. 43.____ ____

44. Gabriel wanted a book **about**
    trains.   44.____ ____

45. **Which** will win the next race?   45.____ ____

46. Will you tell him, **or** shall I?   46.____ ____

47. I gave the **cat** a treat.   47.____ ____

48. His chances seemed **good.**   48.____ ____

49. Listening **and** surveillance
    devices are part of the
    standard equipment.   49.____ ____

50. The first day on a new job is
    always **strange.**   50.____ ____

8. GRAMMAR: COMPLEMENTS

(Study 11B, Complement)

Write in the number that tells how the boldface complement **is used**:

1. direct object	**3. subjective complement**
2. indirect object	**4. objective complement**

Example: Alex and Mallory took the **car**.   ___1___

1.   He has been an **environmentalist** for thirty years.   1._____
2.   My favorite dessert is **ice cream.**   2._____
3.   We gave the **car** a shove.   3._____
4.   He is writing his **memoirs.**   4._____
5.   The logging industry has lost **jobs** to international competitors.   5._____
6.   How can something taste **"light"**?   6._____
7.   Is he the **candidate**?   7._____
8.   Please give **me** your address.   8._____
9.   Alaska made Juneau its **capital**.   9._____
10.   She lent me a **map** of Warsaw.   10._____
11.   Give **me** your solemn promise.   11._____
12.   The student conducted an **experiment**.   12._____
13.   She sounds **happier** every day.   13._____
14.   The mechanic actually reduced the **bill**.   14._____
15.   The university offered **her** a scholarship.   15._____
16.   John installed another **hard drive** on his computer.   16._____
17.   She is a talented basketball **player**.   17._____
18.   Harry is the **judge** for the talent show this year.   18._____
19.   Pamela won a poetry **contest**.   19._____
20.   Have you sent **copies** of the minutes to the members?   20._____
21.   **Whom** did you meet yesterday?   21._____
22.   Who designed the **software**?   22._____
23.   She is a **sophomore** now.   23._____
24.   Will the company give **John** another offer?   24._____
25.   The sun on Malcolm's back felt **good**.   25._____
26.   Politicians will promise **us** anything.   26._____

27. She gave me grandmother's **locket**. 27. _____

28. She is writing an **editorial**. 28. _____

29. The group had been studying **anthropology** for three semesters. 29. _____

30. She has been saving **money** ever since she was eleven years old. 30. _____

31. Either she or I will call **you**. 31. _____

32. Her former employer gave **her** the idea for the small business. 32. _____

33. His proposal sounded **foolish**. 33. _____

34. **Which** did you read first? 34. _____

35. I named him my **beneficiary**. 35. _____

36. Who were the **winners** at the competition? 36. _____

37. She is an **instructor** at the community college. 37. _____

38. She gave **me** no clue regarding her identity. 38. _____

39. That will be **all**, Hudson. 39. _____

40. I bought **tickets** for three games. 40. _____

41. She became an **administrator**. 41. _____

42. I agreed to watch his **children**. 42. _____

43. He considered her a **genius**. 43. _____

44. Select whatever **medium** you like for your art project. 44. _____

45. The company made her **manager** of the branch office. 45. _____

46. Wasn't Eva's sculpture **stunning**? 46. _____

47. Please bake **me** an apple pie. 47. _____

48. Most women don't understand **menopause**. 48. _____

49. The toddler threw her **boots** against the wall. 49. _____

50. The voters gave their leader a **vote** of confidence in the last election. 50. _____

9. GRAMMAR: COMPLEMENTS

(Study 11B, Complement)

Write in the number that tells how the boldface complement **is used:**

1. Direct object   4. subjective complement (noun)
2. Objective complement (noun)   5. subjective complement (pronoun)
3. Objective complement (adjective) 6. subjective complement (adjective)

Example: Hana is a **nurse**.   __4__

1. Anne received an anonymous **letter**.   1.____
2. Jo was **dejected** after the loss.   2.____
3. Hip-hop lyrics are often real-life **stories**. 3.____
4. The music sounded **tuneless**.   4.____
5. Didn't the newspaper provide accurate **coverage**? 5.____
6. Santos named Ahmad his **assistant**.   6.____
7. The jury declared her **guilty**.   7.____
8. Who threw the first **pitch**?   8.____
9. The employment statistics seem **promising**. 9.____
10. Pat has been a **salesperson**.   10.____
11. It was **he** who telephoned.   11.____
12. Close the **door** quietly.   12.____
13. The news story made us **sad**.   13.____
14. The experience was **pleasant**.   14.____
15. Secondhand smoke is **dangerous**.   15.____
16. The campus concert was **boring**.   16.____
17. She is the construction **manager**.   17.____
18. I consider her very **unpleasant**.   18.____
19. He recently bought a **motorcycle**.   19.____
20. Americans are watching less network **television**. 20.____
21. This grant had been her **objective**.   21.____
22. It is **we** who are responsible.   22.____

23. Consider the **impact** on the campus before voting. 23.____
24. I denied that it was **I** who called.   24.____
25. She studies **Japanese** with a tutor.   25.____
26. We consider her **dependable**.   26.____
27. The haunted house attracted curious **people** from all over the state. 27.____
28. He has had great **recognition**.   28.____
29. The news show commentator finally interviewed the reclusive pop **star**. 29.____
30. He did not seem particularly **worried**. 30.____
31. She is **someone** you can trust.   31.____
32. He enjoys ice **fishing**.   32.____
33. She runs a **marathon** each year.   33.____
34. This prescription drug is actually a natural **substance**. 34.____
35. He must have been sound **asleep**.   35.____
36. Alexandra has no **lack** of experience.   36.____
37. Our interest in her career made her very **happy**. 37.____
38. Was it **you** who wrote the essay?   38.____
39. Did you find the **dictionary**?   39.____
40. Are you the chief **nurse**?   40.____
41. Is the victim **anyone** I know?   41.____
42. The speaker advised **everyone** to use alcohol in moderation. 42.____

43. The culprit was **neither** of the employees originally suspected. 43.____

44. His service was **impeccable**. 44.____

45. They made him a good **offer**. 45.____

46. The voters elected her **judge**. 46.____

47. The voters elected **her** judge. 47.____

48. She usually felt **neglected**. 48.____

49. The chess star considered his opponent **stupid**. 49.____

50. Elliot convinced **us** completely. 50.____

10. GRAMMAR: NOUN AND PRONOUN USE

(Study 10-11, Using Nouns; and 19, Use the Right Pronoun Case)

Write the number that tells how each boldface noun or pronoun **is used**.

1. subject	3. indirect object	5. objective complement	7. appositive
2. direct object	4. subjective complement	6. object of preposition	8. direct address

Example: The **marines** stormed the barricades.   ____1____

1. **Packing material** from the box spilled out onto the floor.   1._____

2. Packing material from the **box** spilled out onto the floor.   2._____

3. Some of his fellow **officers** considered Derek somewhat untrustworthy.   3._____

4. Some of his fellow officers considered **Derek** somewhat untrustworthy.   4._____

5. That must have been the **reason** that she told the story.   5._____

6. That must have been the reason that she told the **story**.   6._____

7. His unorthodox behavior made **Singer** the object of criticism.   7._____

8. His unorthodox behavior made Singer the **object** of criticism.   8._____

9. The CIA appointed **Choi** its chief agent for urban rebellions.   9._____

10. The CIA appointed Choi its chief **agent** for urban rebellions.   10._____

11. Mayo, my **supervisor**, requested a detailed report of the students' grades.   11._____

12. Mayo, my supervisor, requested a detailed report of the students' **grades**.   12._____

13. Down the library steps came **Anna**, her arms filled with reference books.   13._____

14. Down the steps came Anna, her arms filled with reference **books**.   14._____

15. She placed his **ring** on a gold chain.   15._____

16. She placed his ring on a gold **chain**.   16._____

17. There are fourteen **students** whom the dean has named campus assistants.   17._____

18. There are fourteen students whom the dean has named campus **assistants**.   18._____

19. Because we've made a commitment to improving race relations on campus, we told the **dean** our concerns.   19._____

20. Because we've made a commitment to improving race relations on campus, we told the dean our **concerns**.   20._____

21. We told our **mother** our concerns about Dad's health.   21._____

22. We told our mother our **concerns** about Dad's health.   22._____

23. Having bought season **tickets**, I saw most of the Indians' games.   23._____

24. Having bought season tickets, I saw **most** of the Indians' games.   24._____

25. First read the **instructions**; then answer the questions carefully.   25._____

26. First read the instructions; then answer the **questions** carefully. 26. _____

27. Harold claimed to know the **combination** to his parents' wall safe. 27. _____

28. Harold claimed to know the combination to his parents' wall **safe**. 28. _____

29. She gave each **student** an opportunity to try out for a part in the play. 29. _____

30. She gave each student an **opportunity** to try out for a part in the play. 30. _____

31. It is, my fellow **students**, time for you to face the problems of apathy at this college. 31. _____

32. It is, my fellow students, time for you to face the **problems** of apathy at this college. 32. _____

33. **Honey**, think about the day we met. 33. _____

34. Honey, think about the **day** we met. 34. _____

35. The club **adviser** invited the members to create a logo for the group. 35. _____

36. The club adviser invited the members to create a **logo** for the group. 36. _____

37. My supervisor appointed **me** the only tutor for the scholarship program. 37. _____

38. My supervisor appointed me the only **tutor** for the scholarship program. 38. _____

39. General Herman's unorthodox **tactics** bewildered the enemy. 39. _____

40. General Herman's unorthodox tactics bewildered the **enemy**. 40. _____

41. The author considers **himself** a successful writer. 41. _____

42. The author considers himself a successful **writer**. 42. _____

43. Dr. Ricardo promised **Sue** that the interview wouldn't be a problem. 43. _____

44. Dr. Ricardo promised Sue that the interview wouldn't be a **problem**. 44. _____

45. There are, **ladies** and gentlemen, many opportunities for safe investments. 45. _____

46. There are, ladies and **gentlemen**, many opportunities for safe investments. 46. _____

47. "Wasn't **he** suspended for drinking in a residence hall?" asked the hall counselor. 47. _____

48. "Wasn't he suspended for drinking in a **residence** hall?" asked the hall counselor. 48. _____

49. We played **tennis** until it was too dark to see the ball. 49. _____

50. We asked the speaker, a former Olympic **medalist**, to discuss physical fitness. 50. _____

11. GRAMMAR: NOUN, PRONOUN, AND ADJECTIVE USE

(Study 4-6, The Parts of Speech: A Survey; 10-11, Using Nouns; and 16, Using Adjectives and Adverbs Correctly)

Instructions: First, write the number (**1** to **3**) of the **part of speech** of the boldface word. Next, write the number (**4** to **9**) that tells how the word **is used.**

1. noun	**4. subject**	**7. subjective complement**
2. pronoun	**5. direct object**	**8. objective complement**
3. adjective	**6. indirect object**	**9. object of preposition**

Example: Music filled the **air**.   _1_ _5_

1. I lent him some **money**.   1._____ ____

2. **Mohammed** made the first team. 2._____ ____

3. She named Sam her **assistant**. 3._____ ____

4. We elected **him** secretary.   4._____ ____

5. Duncan has been a **pilot** for ten years.   5._____ ____

6. The mail was delivered to **her**. 6._____ ____

7. The diplomat was **eager** to begin her new position.   7._____ ____

8. I gave **Sofia** a cupcake.   8._____ ____

9. The report is of interest to **us**. 9._____ ____

10. Our mother always hugged **us** when we upset.   10._____ ____

11. Is **he** the star of the show? 11._____ ____

12. She lives in **Salt Lake City.** 12._____ ____

13. Willy became **depressed** by all his failures.   13._____ ____

14. Will **someone** please help me? 14._____ ____

15. He wrote a **book**.   15._____ ____

16. The President-elect sent **everyone** an invitation.   16._____ ____

17. Her story sounds **plausible**. 17._____ ____

18. Is this **fad** expected to last? 18._____ ____

19. Pablo called me **silly**.   19._____ ____

20. The weather was **mild**.   20._____ ____

21. **Neither** of the soldiers obeyed the order.   21._____ ____

22. We appointed Leo the **manager**. 22._____ ____

23. He became an **administrator**. 23._____ ____

24. Will you buy me a new **stove**? 24._____ ____

25. The only **way** to succeed is to read every day.   25._____ ____

12. GRAMMAR: VERB TENSE

(Study 14A, Know the Three Principal Parts of the Verb; and 14B, Use the Correct Tense of the Verb,)
Write the number of the **tense** of the boldface verb:

1. present   **4. present perfect (have or has)**
2. past   **5. past perfect (had)**
3. future (shall or will)   **6. future perfect (shall have or will have)**

Example: You **spoke** too soon.   _2_

1. The sun **sets** in the west.   1.____

2. He **will** surely **write** us soon.   2.____

3. Next summer, we **shall have lived**
    in this house for ten years.   3.____

4. The Allens **have planted** a vegetable
    garden.   4.____

5. By noon he **will have finished** the
    whole job.   5.____

6. Here **is** the six o'clock news.   6.____

7. **Shall** we **reserve** a copy for you?   7.____

8. The widow's savings **melted** away.   8.____

9. I **had** not **expected** to see her.   9.____

10. Aaron **likes** to play with clay.   10.____

11. The company **guaranteed** that the
    package would arrive in the morning. 11.____

12. Dylan **will begin** cello lessons in
    the spring.   12.____

13. The children **have created** a snow
    castle in the front yard.   13.____

14. **Have** you an extra set of car keys? 14.____

15. My eighty-four-year-old father **loves**
    to   his   motorcycle   on
    mountain roads.   15.____

16. I **wrote** a review of the school play. 16.____

17. The family **has planned** a vacation. 17.____

18. The comic **laughed** at his own jokes. 18.____

19. In one week the flu **hit** five staff
    members.   19.____

20. Michael **has applied** for a junior
    year abroad.   20.____

Write the number of the **verb ending,** if any, that should appear at each bracketed space:

0. no ending   **1. s or es**   **2. ed or d**   **3. ing**

Example: The sun rise[ ] beyond that low hill.   _____2____

The brown cliffs rise[1] directly from the gray sea; no beach come[2] between them. The   1._____

waves have pound[3] the granite base of that cliff for ages but have fail[4] to wear[5] it away.   2._____

Now, as always, great white gulls circle[6] just above the foam seeking fish that are   3._____

destine[7] to become their dinner. Years ago, when I first gather[8] the courage to approach[9]   4._____

the cliff's sheer edge and peer[10] over, I imagine[11] what it would be like if I tumble[12] over   5._____

and plummet[13] into that seething surf. I was an imaginative youth, and the thought   6._____

fascinate[14] me then. At that time I was try[15] desperately though unsuccessfully to win the

heart of a dark-haired local young woman, but she had been continually reject[16] me,

and her attitude had turn[17] my thoughts to suicide. I might, in fact, have hurl[18] myself

over the edge, except for one fact. My knees have always turn[19] to jelly at the mere

thought of do[20] it. Today, as a man of thirty, I can look[21] back on those years and

laugh[22]. Yet even now, whenever I approach[23] that treacherous edge, a chill run[24]

through me. It is as if something inside me is say[25], "Someday you will hurl[26] yourself

over. You know[27] it." I have been haunt[28] by that thought ever since that woman reject[29]

me, and I probably will always be obsess[30] by it—until the end.

7. _____

8. _____

9. _____

10. _____

11. _____

12. _____

13. _____

14. _____

15. _____

16. _____

17. _____

18. _____

19. _____

20. _____

21. _____

22. _____

23. _____

24. _____

25. _____

26. _____

27. _____

28. _____

29. _____

30. _____

13. GRAMMAR: VERBS—KIND, VOICE, AND MOOD

(Study 13, Know the Kinds of Verbs)

Write **1** if the boldface verb is **transitive**.
Write **2** if it is **intransitive**.
Write **3** if it is a **linking** verb.

Example: The house **looks** fine.   __3__

1. Jenny **kissed** me when we met.   1.____
2. Gerald **jogs** for two miles every morning.   2.____
3. His laughter **sounded** bitter.   3.____
4. **Lay** your wet coat by the furnace.   4.____
5. The window **opened** onto the bay.   5.____
6. Dr. Smiley **has** a fine reputation.   6.____
7. The island **lies** fifty miles off the mainland.   7.____
8. The last express **has** already **left**.   8.____
9. **Place** the keys on my dresser.   9.____
10. The childhood playmates **remained** friends for life.   10.____
11. The kitchen **smells** good.   11.____
12. The book **seems** too complicated.   12.____
13. The plane **arrived** ten minutes late.   13.____
14. The mail carrier **left** a package.   14.____
15. The snow **piled** up into tall, crusty drifts.   15.____
16. We **visited** my family's homestead last July.   16.____
17. The boys **created** valentines for their teachers, friends and family.   17.____
18. My friend **seemed** nervous.   18.____
19. The young teacher **was** a former student in my first class.   19.____
20. Women **have been** instrumental in maintaining the social structure of the American Protestant churches.   20.____

Write **1** if the boldface verb is in the **active** voice.
Write **2** if it is in the **passive** voice.

Example: Lefty **threw** another strike.   __1__

1. Visitors **are** not **permitted** aboard the aircraft.   1.____
2. One name **was** inadvertently omitted from the list.   2.____
3. The negotiator **carried** a special agreement to the union meeting.   3.____
4. The media **bashed** the incumbent's speech.   4.____
5. The meeting **was called** to order.   5.____
6. The ancient city **was** totally **destroyed** by a volcanic eruption.   6.____
7. An accounting error **was discovered**.   7.____
8. Younger voters **have selected** their presidential candidate.   8.____
9. The witness **faltered** under the vigorous cross-examination.   9.____
10. The theft **could have occurred** early in the morning.   10.____
11. The status report **will be submitted** next week.   11.____
12. The left fielder **threw out** the runner.   12.____
13. Jorge's credit card application **was approved.**   13.____

14. The movie star's exercise video **will be sold** through half-hour commercials. 14.____

15. I **baked** my husband's favorite dessert for Father's Day. 15.____

Write the number of the **mood** of the boldface verb:

1. indicative   2. imperative   3. subjunctive

Example: If she **were** smart, she'd finis school first. ___1___

1. The semester **had ended.** 1.____

2. They **are** lovers. 2.____

3. **Kiss** me, you fool! 3.____

4. The research team **is conducting** another set of experiments. 4.____

5. Would that I **were** wealthy. 5.____

6. **Send** my check to the bank. 6.____

7. If I **were** you, I'd not worry. 7.____

8. **Drive** carefully in snowy weather. 8.____

9. Dean **gave** us some candy. 9.____

10. Please **read** the directions twice before beginning. 10.____

11. The students **were** tired from studying. 11.____

12. They were **late** as usual. 12.____

13. **Look out!** 13.____

14. The student **hurried** to finish his math test. 14.____

15. If this **be** treason, make the most of it. 15.____

14. GRAMMAR: VERBALS

(Study 14D, Distinguish a Verbal from a Verb)

Identify **each** boldface verbal by selecting the correct number:

1. infinitive   **3. present participle**
2. gerund   **4. past participle**

Example: **To be** or not to be; that is the
question.   1

1. Do you like **to watch** football?   1.____

2. Her hobby is **remodeling** her home.   2.____

3. The President's first job was **to restore**
the economy for all Americans.   3.____

4. Our **laughing** distracted him.   4.____

5. I submitted a **typed** application.   5.____

6. **Encouraged** by their initial weight
loss, Cecilia and Roy continued
their diets.   6.____

7. He was eager **to start** an exercise
program.   7.____

8. By **surveying** the chapter, he knew
what he needed to learn.   8.____

9. **Seeing** us, she smiled.   9.____

10. She enjoys **driving** sports cars.   10.____

11. Seismologists continue **to monitor**
California for a really powerful
earthquake.   11.____

12. **Examining** the report, the consumer
decided not to invest.   12.____

13. **Frightened**, he became cautious.   13.____

14. The purpose of the cookbook is **to
reduce** the threat of cancer through
a healthful diet.   14.____

15. **Reducing** carbon dioxide emissions
was a top priority in a recent bill.   15.____

Identify the boldface verbal in two ways. First, write the number that classifies the phrase as either
(1) **an infinitive phrase,** or (2) a **gerund phrase.**

Next, write the number that shows how the boldface verbal is used:
(3) **subject**; (4) **direct object**; (5) **subjective complement**; or (6) **object of preposition.**

Example: Sleeping until noon is no way to greet the day   2   1

1. The professor clearly enjoyed **reading** her favorite passages to the class.   1.____ ____

2. **To blame** Governor Riley completely for the weak economy is a rather naive viewpoint.   2.____ ____

3. Lorie likes **working** with young children in summer camp.   3.____ ____

4. The ambassador's first task was **to arrange** a summit meeting.   4.____ ____

5. The suspect apparently had no intention of **admitting** the crime.   5.____ ____

6. Kirsten thought about **traveling** to Mexico over break.   6.____ ____

7. We tried **to stop** him from making an unwise decision.   7.____ ____

8. Her one wish has always been **to write** a romance novel. 8. ____ ____

9. **Conducting** the field study was fascinating. 9. ____ ____

10. The central characteristic of aboriginal discourse is the **monitoring** of the progress of any discussion. 10. ____ ____

15. GRAMMAR: ADJECTIVES AND ADVERBS

(Study 16-17, Using Adjectives and Adverbs)

Write **1** if the boldface adjective or adverb is used **correctly**.
Write **2** if it used **incorrectly**.

Example: The Cardinals are playing **good** this year.   _2_

1. The sun feels **good**.   1.____
2. The team shouldn't feel **badly** about losing that game.   2.____
3. She was the **most** talented member of the dance couple.   3.____
4. He keeps in **good** condition always.   4.____
5. He was very **frank** in his evaluation of his work.   5.____
6. My father spoke very **frankly** with us.   6.____
7. Of the two students, she is the **smartest**.   7.____
8. My leg aches **bad**.   8.____
9. The student looked **cheerful**.   9.____
10. The student looked **wearily** at the computer monitor.   10.____
11. I comb my hair **different** now.   11.____
12. Was the deer hurt **bad**?   12.____
13. He seemed **real** sad.   13.____
14. The Learning Assistant tried **awful** hard to keep the residence hall quiet during finals week.   14.____
15. Reading Eudora Welty's work is a **real** pleasure.   15.____
16. The teaching assistant glanced **nervously** at the class.   16.____
17. The bus driver seemed **nervous**.   17.____
18. The campus will look **differently** when the new buildings are completed.   18.____

19. Yours is the **clearest** of the two explanations.   19.____
20. The book is in **good** condition.   20.____
21. I did **poor** in organic chemistry this term.   21.____
22. Mario looked **debonair** in his new suit.   22.____
23. Trevor felt **badly** about having to fire the veteran employee.   23.____
24. Daryl's excuse was far **more poorer** than Keith's.   24.____
25. She writes very **well**.   25.____
26. It rained **steady** for the whole month of December in Houston.   26.____
27. The roses smell **sweet**.   27.____
28. He tries **hard** to please everyone.   28.____
29. John is **near** seven feet tall.   29.____
30. He talks **considerable** about his career plans.   30.____
31. She donated a **considerable** sum of money to the project.   31.____
32. The **smartest** of the twins is spoiled. 32.____
33. The **smartest** of the triplets is spoiled.   33.____
34. The coach gazed **uneasily** at her players.   34.____
35. He felt **uneasy** about the score.   35.____
36. Do try to drive more **careful**.   36.____
37. It was Bob's **most unique** idea ever.   37.____
38. The trial was **highly** publicized.   38.____

39. Larry arrived **considerable** later than the others. 39.____

40. The house looked **strangely** to us. 40.____

41. The software has run **good** since the computer viruses were removed. 41.____

42. He was ill, but he is **well** now. 42.____

43. That lobbyist is the most **influential** in Washington. 43.____

44. The orchestra sounded **good** throughout the hall. 44.____

45. Societal violence has **really** reached epidemic proportions in this country. 45.____

46. He seemed very **serious** about changing jobs. 46.____

47. The egg rolls smelled **good**. 47.____

48. We felt **badly** about missing the farewell party. 48.____

49. Rafael looked on **sadly**. 49.____

50. Paul was **sad** all morning. 50.____

16. GRAMMAR: USING VERBS

(Study 15D, Do Not Misuse Irregular Verb Forms)

Write **1** if the boldface verb is used **correctly**.
Write **0** if it is used **incorrectly**; then write in the correct verb form.

Example: We were **froze** by the time we shoveled the driveway.   <u>0</u>   <u>frozen</u>

1.   I **payed** the news carrier.   1.___ _____

2.   We have **flown** home to Wyoming four times this year.   2.___ _____

3.   In the summer, we **swam** in the creek behind our home.   3.___ _____

4.   The bell in Clark Tower has **rang** every evening at 6:00 p.m. for the past fifty years. 4.___ _____

5.   My hat was **stole** when I left it at the restaurant.   5.___ _____

6.   We have **ridden** the train to Chicago many times.   6.___ _____

7.   The little child **tore** open the present wrapped in bright yellow paper.   7.___ _____

8.   The student **sunk** into his chair to avoid being called on by the professor. 8.___ _____

9.   We have **gone** to the county fair every year since we moved to San Antonio. 9.___ _____

10. We should have **known** that Robert would be late for the meeting.   10.___ _____

11. The little boy standing by the counter **seen** the man shoplift a watch.   11.___ _____

12. Before we realized it, we had **drank** two pitchers of lemonade.   12.___ _____

13. The team **rose** at 4:00 a.m. to prepare for their tournament.   13.___ _____

14. The medals **shone** brightly on the general's uniform.   14.___ _____

15. The children **swang** on the swing until their mother called them home for supper. 15.___ _____

16. When we were small, we **wore** hats and white gloves on special occasions. 16.___ _____

17. The author hasn't **spoken** to the news media for fifty years.   17.___ _____

18. Jack **wrote** his essay on the summer spent on his grandfather's farm.   18.___ _____

19. We **lay** on the couch reading the Sunday newspaper and munching donuts. 19.___ _____

20. Jack **stole** the chocolate candy when his brother left the kitchen.   20.___ _____

Name _____ Class _____ Date _____ Score (R_____ x 4)_____

17. GRAMMAR: PRONOUNS—KINDS AND CASE

(Study 18, Know the Five Main Kinds of Pronouns; and 19, Use the Right Pronoun Case.)

Classify each boldface pronoun by selecting the correct number below:

1. personal pronoun
2. interrogative pronoun
3. relative pronoun
4. demonstrative pronoun

5. indefinite pronoun
6. reflexive pronoun
7. intensive pronoun

Example: Who is Sylvia? _____2_____

1. I made him an offer that **he** could not refuse. 1._____
2. **No one** believed Albert's latest reason for missing work. 2._____
3. **This** supports the importance of proper rest when studying for finals. 3._____
4. He has only **himself** to blame for his predicament. 4._____
5. **Which** of the city newspapers do you read? 5._____
6. She is the executive **who** makes the key decisions in this company. 6._____
7. I **myself** have no desire to explore the rough terrain of mountainous regions. 7._____
8. **Everyone** promised to be on time for the staff meeting. 8._____
9. **Several** of the players complained about the heat. 9._____
10. **Anyone** seeing his latest documentary will want to join a volunteer program. 10._____
11. Dean prepared a speech in case **someone** actually showed up for the workshop. 11._____
12. These are my biology notes; **those** must be yours. 12._____
13. **Who** do you think will win the poetry contest? 13._____
14. **Each** of the generals offered testimony. 14._____
15. **Neither** of the organizations worked on increasing membership. 15._____

Write the number of the **correct** pronoun choice.

Example: Grandpa ordered lunch for Billy and (1)**I** (2)**me.** _____2_____

1. Three of (1)**we** (2)**us** jury members voted for acquittal. 1._____
2. Although I tried to be careful around the cat, I still stepped on (1)**its** (2)**it's** tail three times. 2._____
3. May we—John and (1)**I** (2)**me**—join you for the meeting? 3._____
4. Between you and (1)**I** (2)**me**, I feel quite uneasy about the outcome of the expedition. 4._____
5. Were you surprised that the book was written by Jake and (1)**he** (2)**him**? 5._____

·39

6. It must have been (1)**he** (2)**him** who wrote the article about plant safety for the company newsletter.

7. Why not support (1)**we** (2)**us** students in our efforts to have a new student union?

8. No one except (1)**she** (2)**her** could figure out the copier machine.

9. He is much more talented in dramatics than (1)**she** (2)**her**.

10. The audience cheered (1)**whoever** (2)**whomever** made fun of the mayor and his city council.

18. GRAMMAR: PRONOUN CASE

(Study 19, Use the Right Pronoun Case)

First, write in the number of the **correct** pronoun choice.
Next, write in the number of the **reason** for your choice.

Choice

(1) subject form (nominative case)

(2) object form (objective case)

Reason

(3) subject of verb
(4) subjective complement
(5) direct object
(6) indirect object
(7) object of preposition
(8) subject of infinitive

Example: Marie studied with Burt and (1)**I** (2)**me**.   2   7

1. Do you think it was (1)**she** (2)**her** who poisoned the cocoa?   1.____ ____

2. Were you and (1)**he** (2)**him** ever in Montana?   2.____ ____

3. Fourteen of (1)**we** (2)**us** students signed a petition to reverse the ruling.   3.____ ____

4. The assignment gave (1)**she** (2)**her** no further trouble after it was explained.   4.____ ____

5. Sam Lewis preferred to be remembered as the person (1)**who** (2)**whom** invented the jalapeno-flavored lollipop.   5.____ ____

6. I invited (1)**he** (2)**him** to select topics on which students might speak.   6.____ ____

7. Speakers like (1)**she** (2)**her** are both entertaining and informative.   7.____ ____

8. I was very much surprised to see (1)**he** (2)**him** at the art exhibit.   8.____ ____

9. Have you and (1)**he** (2)**him** completed your research on the origins of American rodeos?   9.____ ____

10. We asked Joan and (1)**he** (2)**him** to supervise the playground activities.   10.____ ____

11. The leader of the student group asked, "(1)**Who** (2)**Whom** can afford the 10 percent increase in tuition?"   11.____ ____

12. All of (1)**we** (2)**us** tourists spent the entire afternoon in a roadside museum.   12.____ ____

13. It was (1)**he** (2)**him** who made all the arrangements for the dance.   13.____ ____

14. Television network executives seem to think that ratings go to (1)**whoever** (2)**whomever** broadcasts the sexiest shows.   14.____ ____

15. My two friends and (1)**I** (2)**me** decided to visit Window Rock, Arizona, headquarters of the Navajo nation.   15.____ ____

16. This argument is just between Dick and (1)**I** (2)**me**.   16.____ ____

17. My father always gave (1)**I** (2)**me** money for my tuition.   17.____ ____

18. The cowboy movie star offered to co-produce a movie with (1)**whoever** (2)**whomever** promised an accurate portrayal of his life.

18. ____ ____

19. If you were (1)**I** (2)**me**, would you consider going on a summer cruise?

19. ____ ____

20. Please ask (1)**whoever** (2)**whomever** is at the door to wait.

20. ____ ____

21. Everyone was excused from class except Louise, Mary, and (1)**I** (2)**me**.

21. ____ ____

22. The teaching assistant asked (1)**he** (2)**him** to finish the experiment.

22. ____ ____

23. Nina was as interested as (1)**he** (2)**him** in moving to Florida after their retirement.

23. ____ ____

24. I knew of no one who had encountered more difficulties than (1)**she** (2)**her**.

24. ____ ____

25. Monisha gave (1)**I** (2)**me** the summary for our report.

25. ____ ____

26. Our child's teacher asked (1)**we** (2)**us** to consider meeting with an educational consultant.

26. ____ ____

27. The dance instructor was actually fifteen years older than (1)**he** (2)**him**.

27. ____ ____

28. Fifty of (1)**we** (2)**us** agreed to raise money for a memorial plaque.

28. ____ ____

29. Are you and (1)**she** (2)**her** planning a joint report?

29. ____ ____

30. It is (1)**I** (2)**me** who is charge of the bake sales for my children's school.

30. ____ ____

31. I am certain that he is as deserving of praise as (1)**she** (2)**her**.

31. ____ ____

32. If you were (1)**I** (2)**me**, where would you spend spring break?

32. ____ ____

33. (1)**Who** (2)**Whom** do you think will be the next mayor?

33. ____ ____

34. Assign the project to (1)**whoever** (2)**whomever** doesn't mind traveling.

34. ____ ____

35. She is a person (1)**who** (2)**whom** is, without question, destined to achieve success.

35. ____ ____

36. He is the author about (1)**who** (2)**whom** we shall be writing a paper.

36. ____ ____

37. Was it (1)**he** (2)**him** who won the contest?

37. ____ ____

38. The only choice left was between (1)**she** (2)**her** and him.

38. ____ ____

39. No one actually read the book except (1)**she** (2)**her**.

39. ____ ____

40. "Were you calling (1)**I** (2)**me**?" Jill asked as she entered the room.

40. ____ ____

41. Both of (1)**we** (2)**us** agreed that the exercise class was scheduled at an inconvenient time.

41. ____ ____

42. Imagine finally meeting (1)**he** (2)**him** after so many years of correspondence!

42. ____ ____

43. The researcher asked both the mayor and (1)**she** (2)**her** about issues surrounding the renovation of the football stadium.

43. ____ ____

44. Do you suppose that (1)**he** (2)**him** will ever find time to come?

44. ____ ____

45. Jose sent an invitation to (1)**I** (2)**me**.

45. ____ ____

46. It was the other reviewer who disliked the movie, not (1)**I** (2)**me**.

46. ____ ____

47. Developing an anti-bias school curriculum gave our colleagues and (1)**we** (2)**us** much satisfaction.

47. ____ ____

48. A dispute arose about (1)**who** (2)**whom** would arrange the conference call.

48. ____ ____

49. That executive is the one (1)**who** (2)**whom** initiated the investigation.

49. ____ ____

50. The contracts will be given to (1)**whoever** (2)**whomever** prepares the most complete proposal.

50. ____ ____

19. GRAMMAR: PRONOUN REFERENCE

(Study 20, Avoid Faulty Reference)

Write **1** if the boldface word is used **correctly**.
Write **0** if it is used **incorrectly**.

Example: Gulliver agreed with his master that **he** was a Yahoo. _____0_____

1. David won the lottery and quit his job. **This** was unexpected. 1._____

2. Jane told Monisha that **she** wasn't ready for the chemistry test. 2._____

3. Daniel decided to drop out of college. He later regretted **that** decision. 3._____

4. On the white card, list the classes **that** you plan to take. 4._____

5. The veteran football player practiced with the rookie because **he** wanted to review the new plays. 5._____

6. In Buffalo, **they** eat chicken wings served with blue cheese dressing and celery. 6._____

7. I was late filing my report, **which** greatly embarrassed me. 7._____

8. In the United States, **they** mail approximately 166 billion letters and packages each year. 8._____

9. She was able to complete college after earning a research assistantship. We greatly admire her for **that**. 9._____

10. The physician's speech focused on the country's lack of attention to the AIDS epidemic; **it** was not well received. 10._____

11. According to my Native American grandfather, a real Indian is one who knows and respects the ways of **his** ancestors. 11._____

12. They planned to climb sheer Mount Maguffey, a feat **that** no one had ever accomplished. 12._____

13. Pat always wanted to be a television newscaster; thus she majored in **it** in college. 13._____

14. The average American child watches over thirty hours of television each week, **which** is why we are no longer a nation of readers. 14._____

15. **It** was well past midnight when the phone rang. 15._____

16. The speaker kept scratching his head, a mannerism **that** proved distracting. 16._____

17. **It** says in the magazine story that the youngest person to receive an Oscar was ten-year-old Tatum O'Neal. 17._____

18. When Dan drives down the street in his red sports car, **they** all look on with admiration and, perhaps, just a little envy. 18._____

19. Aaron told Evan that **he** couldn't play in the soccer game. 19._____

20. Eric started taking pictures in high school. **This** interest led to a brilliant career in photography. 20._____

21. **It** is best to be aware of both the caloric and fat content of food in your diet. 21._____

22. In some vacation spots, **they** add the tip to your bill and give poor service. This isn't the way to treat a customer.

22. _____

23. In some vacation spots, they add the tip to your bill and give poor service. **This** isn't the way to treat a customer.

23. _____

24. In some sections of the history text, **it** seems as if they ignored women's contributions to the development of this country.

24. _____

25. In some sections of the history text, it seems as if **they** ignored women's contributions to the development of this country.

25. _____

20. GRAMMAR: PHRASES

(Study 21-22, Recognizing Phrases)

First, write the number of the **one** set of words that is a **prepositional phrase**.
Second, write the number that tells how that phrase is **used** in that sentence:

7. as adjective   **8. as adverb**

Example: The starting pitcher for the Dodgers is a left-hander.   <u>2</u>   <u>7</u>
      1   2   3

1.   When we came downstairs, a cab was awaiting us at the curb.   1. ____ ____
         1   2   3   4

2.   The red-brick building erected in the last century collapsed last week
         1   2   3

     without warning.   2. ____ ____
         4

3.   The lady with the fur stole is actually married to an animal activist.   3. ____ ____
       1   2   3   4

4.   What they saw before the door closed shocked them beyond belief.   4. ____ ____
       1   2   3   4

5.   The most frequently used word in the English language is the word the.   5. ____ ____
             1   2   3

6.   The need for adequate child care for dual-income families was not
       1   2   3

     considered when the President addressed the convention.   6. ____ ____

7.   The observation that men and women have different courtship rituals
       1   2

     seems debatable in a modern postindustrial society.   7. ____ ____
       3   4

8.   At our yard sale, I found out that people will buy almost anything
         1   2

     if the price is right.   8. ____ ____
         3

9.   Until 10,000 years ago, all humans relied on food gathering and hunting
         1   2

     to maintain their existence.   9. ____ ____
         3

10. Although skateboarding is a relatively new sport, there have been
              1   2

     world championships staged since 1966.   10. ____ ____
         3   4

If the words in boldface are **a verbal phrase** (infinitive, gerund or participial), write **1** then write one of the following numbers:

2. verbal phrase used as **adjective**
3. verbal phrase used as **adverb**
4. verbal phrase used as **noun**.

If the boldface words **are not a verbal phrase,** write **0** only.

Example: Singing in the rain is a sure way to get wet.   <u> 1 </u> <u> 4 </u>

Example: Gene is **singing in the rain** despite his cold.   <u> 0 </u> <u>   </u>

1. **Taking portrait photographs of pets** is her means of earning a living.   1. ____ ____

2. Now she is **taking portrait photographs of pets** as her means of earning a living.   2. ____ ____

3. **To prepare his income taxes,** Sam spent several hours sorting through the shoe boxes filled with receipts.   3. ____ ____

4. By age 30, many women begin **sensing a natural maternal need.**   4. ____ ____

5. A successful high school athlete, **courted by major universities,** sometimes receives substantial cash gifts from athletic booster clubs.   5. ____ ____

6. English departments are debating the issue of **forsaking a Eurocentric curriculum for a more multicultural approach.**   6. ____ ____

7. His idea of a thrill is **driving in stock-car races.**   7. ____ ____

8. **Driving in stock-car races,** he not only gets his thrills but also earns prize money.   8. ____ ____

9. The minister is **attempting to collect money for a special project.**   9. ____ ____

10. He would like **to build his own home someday.**   10. ____ ____

21. GRAMMAR: VERBAL PHRASES

(Study 22, The Verbal Phrase)

Classify each boldface verbal phrase by writing in the correct numbers as listed below.

1. **infinitive phrase** used as a noun
2. **infinitive phrase** used as adjective
3. **infinitive phrase** used as adverb
4. **present participial** phrase
5. **past participial** phrase
6. **gerund phrase**

Example: **Thrilled by her results,** Elaine began applying to several colleges.   _____5_____

Example: Thrilled by her results, Elaine began **applying to several colleges.**   _____6_____

1. **Seeing the traffic worsen,** Adam chose to wait until after rush hour.   1._____

2. Seeing the traffic worsen, Adam chose **to wait until after rush hour.**   2._____

3. **Buying even one ticket to an Indians' game** was difficult to do.   3._____

4. Buying even one ticket to an Indians' game was difficult **to do.**   4._____

5. **Controlling acid rain** is a crucial step in protecting our lakes and rivers.   5._____

6. Controlling acid rain is a crucial step in **protecting our lakes and rivers.**   6._____

7. **Intrigued by what he was saying,** she forgot to go to her science class.   7._____

8. Intrigued by what he was saying, she forgot **to go to her science class.**   8._____

9. **Realizing the importance of financial planning**, David decided to make an appointment with an investment counselor.   9._____

10. Realizing the importance of financial planning, David decided **to make an appointment with an investment counselor.**   10._____

11. **To provide safe neighborhoods** is the mayor's first task facing her after inauguration.   11._____

12. To provide safe neighborhoods is the mayor's first task **facing her after inauguration.**   12._____

13. I can't help **liking her** even though she isn't interested in understanding my point of view.   13._____

14. I can't help liking her even though she isn't interested in **understanding my point of view.**   14._____

15. I appreciate **your helping us**; will you be able to help us again?   15._____

16. I appreciate your helping us: will you be able **to help us again**?   16._____

17. **Loaded down with library books,** she tried to open the front door.   17._____

18. Loaded down with library books, she tried **to open the front door.**   18._____

19. **Reading my psychology assignment** was easy because it was about communicating with older people.

19. _____

20. Reading my psychology assignment was easy because it was about **communicating with older people.**

20. _____

21. **Realizing the importance of keeping my car repaired,** I promised to change the oil frequently.

21. _____

22. Realizing the importance of keeping my car repaired, I promised **to change the oil more frequently.**

22. _____

23. Garcia tried **to run the whole mile,** but he was too tired to do more than a single lap.

23. _____

24. Garcia tried to run the whole mile, but he was too tired **to do more than a single lap.**

24. _____

25. The speaker, **obviously resenting our interruptions,** frowned at us as we tried to ask other questions.

25. _____

26. The speaker, obviously resenting our interruptions, frowned at us as we tried **to ask other questions.**

26. _____

27. **Hiking over mountain trails** is a sport demanding endurance.

27. _____

28. Hiking over mountain trails is a sport **demanding endurance.**

28. _____

29. The hunter put down his gun, **realizing that the ducks had flown out of range** and wishing to save ammunition.

29. _____

30. The hunter put down his gun, realizing that the ducks had flown out of range and **wishing to save ammunition.**

30. _____

31. To try to pass the test without **studying for it** was not a wise thing to do.

31. _____

32. To try to pass the test without studying for it was not a wise thing **to do.**

32. _____

33. **Concerned about the level of violence in our community,** Al organized a group of senior citizens to watch out for one another.

33. _____

34. Concerned about the level of violence in our community, Al organized a group of senior citizens **to watch out for one another.**

34. _____

35. **Feeling guilty about working outside of the home,** the young mother planned to spend time with her children every Saturday.

35. _____

36. Feeling guilty about working outside of the home, the young mother planned **to spend time with her children every Saturday.**

36. _____

37. **Drinking chlorinated water** may be linked to increasing the risk of rectal and bladder cancer.

37. _____

38. Drinking chlorinated water may be linked to **increasing the risk of rectal and bladder cancer.**

38. _____

39. She tried **to obtain the information** without asking any direct questions.

39. _____

40. She tried to obtain the information without **asking any direct questions.**

40. _____

41. The student **waiting in your office** has to select a major this semester.

41. _____

42. The student waiting in your office has **to select a major this semester.**

42. _____

43. **Being careless with campfires** has been the cause of too many forests being reduced to ashes.

43. _____

44. The book **to read** is one that helps you to escape daily tension.

44. _____

45. **By looking carefully**, he found an article that was easy to understand.   45. _____

46. By looking carefully, he found an article that was easy **to understand**.   46. _____

47. **Obviously surprised by the sacrifices required**, Gina reconsidered whether she wanted to begin gymnastic training for the next Olympics.   47. _____

48. Obviously surprised by the sacrifices required, Gina reconsidered whether she wanted **to begin gymnastic training for the next Olympics**.   48. _____

49. **To be extremely safe**, physicians are recommending that patients preparing for any surgery donate blood.   49. _____

50. To be extremely safe, physicians are recommending that patients **preparing for any surgery** donate blood.   50. _____

22. GRAMMAR: PHRASES—REVIEW

(Study 21-22, Recognizing Phrases)

Classify each boldface phrase by writing in the correct number:

1. prepositional phrase 4. gerund phrase
2. infinitive phrase   5. absolute phrase
3. participial phrase

Then decide how that phrase is used and write in the correct number:
6. as adjective   7. as adverb   8. as noun

(For an absolute phrase, do **not** write a number to tell how the phrase was used.)

Example: The orders came **from on high**.   1   7

1.   The woman standing **between the delegates** is an interpreter.   1.____ ____

2.   The woman **standing between the delegates** is an interpreter.   2.____ ____

3.   The first televisions had small round screens encased **in large wooden cabinets.**   3.____ ____

4.   **His insisting that he was right** made him unpopular with his associates.   4.____ ____

5.   The committee voted **to adjourn immediately.**   5.____ ____

6.   **Because of the storm**, the excursion around the lake had to be postponed.   6.____ ____

7.   **To stay awake in Smedley's class** required dedication and a lot of black coffee.   7.____ ____

8.   **During television programming in the 1940s**, many commercials were five minutes long.   8.____ ____

9.   **Flying a jet at supersonic speeds** has been Sally's dream since childhood.   9.____ ____

10. The agent **wearing an official badge** is the one to see about tickets.   10.____ ____

11. **Realizing that his back injury would get worse**, the star player retired from professional basketball.   11.____ ____

12. **To pay for their dream vacation**, Harry and Sue both took on extra jobs.   12.____ ____

13. **To assist students with their course schedules**, counselors will be on duty all day.   13.____ ____

14. The children were successful in **developing their own lawn-mowing company.**   14.____ ____

15. **The semester completed**, students were packing up to go home.   15.____ ____

16. The distinguished-looking man **in the blue suit** is the head of the company.   16.____ ____

17. **Earning a college degree** used to guarantee a well-paying job.   17.____ ____

18. Approximately one-fourth **of the American work force** has a college degree.   18.____ ____

19. On May 11, 1939, the first baseball game was telecast **in America.**   19.____ ____

20. Deciding which car **to buy** is a difficult task.   20.____ ____

21. Two crates **of oranges** were delivered to the fraternity house. 21. ____ ____

22. **Anticipating an overflow audience**, the custodian put extra chairs in the auditorium. 22. ____ ____

23. A car **filled with students** left early this morning to arrange for the class picnic. 23. ____ ____

24. The woman **with the large, floppy hat** is my eccentric aunt. 24. ____ ____

25. We were obliged to abandon our plans, **the boat having been damaged in a recent storm.** 25. ____ ____

26. We knew, **conditions being what they were**, that further progress was impossible. 26. ____ ____

27. **Doing my homework** interfered with my watching television. 27. ____ ____

28. **Waving his arms and shouting,** John threatened everyone in the courtroom. 28. ____ ____

29. **Flipping through the channels**, Fred decided that reading the phone book would be more interesting than watching television. 29. ____ ____

30. **His book having been published**, Dylan planned a long vacation. 30. ____ ____

31. Scientists are using artificial life simulation programs **for futuristic experimentation.** 31. ____ ____

32. **Having visited Two Eggs, Florida**, Sam headed for Who'd A Thought It, Alabama. 32. ____ ____

33. **Realizing that the Broadway tickets would be over $100**, John and Tina decided to see a movie instead. 33. ____ ____

34. **Backing up all computer files** was something she seldom did. 34. ____ ____

35. **Realizing that the state motto was sexist**, the state legislators provided a more modern version. 35. ____ ____

36. North America, Asia, and Europe must work together **to prevent the holes in the ozone layer from becoming any larger.** 36. ____ ____

37. The international community, **changing with the fall of the Soviet Union**, has revamped its undercover operations. 37. ____ ____

38. Philo Farnsworth invented the concept of television while still **in his teens.** 38. ____ ____

39. **Growing tired of the violence and sex in most movies**, many parents' groups are protesting at local theaters. 39. ____ ____

40. Almost 80 percent of those Americans **polled recently** believed that with enough determination and talent, anyone can be successful in this country. 40. ____ ____

41. **Being part of an extended family** is important to many Hawaiian societies. 41. ____ ____

42. As societies become more industrialized, the benefits **of raising small families** outweigh having large families. 42. ____ ____

43. **Until the 1700s**, the white potato plant was grown strictly as an ornamental plant in Europe. 43. ____ ____

44. **To listen to radio broadcasts in the 1920s**, Americans often used a homemade crystal set. 44. ____ ____

45. **Consuming more than 50 pounds of ground beef each year**, Americans annually buy 6.7 billion hamburger patties at fast-food restaurants. 45. ____ ____

46. **The weekend shot**, Albino decided to go to bed early even though he had more schoolwork to complete. 46. ____ ____

47. American widows, **reporting that friends and relatives interfere too much**, frequently prefer to spend time alone. 47. ____ ____

48. Anthropologists explain cultural variations **by discussing the impact that ecological and societal functions have on people.**   48. ____ ____

49. **To demonstrate a sense of humility** is important in verbal communication among Chinese speakers.   49. ____ ____

50. **Trudging through the heavy rainstorm**, James vowed to buy an umbrella that night.   50. ____ ____

23. GRAMMAR: CLAUSES

(Study 23-25, Recognizing Clauses)

Classify each boldface clause by writing the correct number:

1. independent (main) clause   2. adjective clause
3. adverb clause   } [2, 3, & 4 are classified as
4. noun clause   } dependent (subordinate) clauses]

Example: Do the dishes **when you're finished eating.**   ___3___

1. Day-care employees complain **because there is no economic incentive to stay in the field.**   1._____

2. The governor considered the latest proposal, **which called for local police units to work more closely with school districts.**   2._____

3. Late-night television viewers know **how the comedian begins his monologue.**   3._____

4. The student **who made the top grade in the history quiz** is my roommate.   4._____

5. **Whether I am able to go to college** depends on whether I can find employment.   5._____

6. **After Judd had written a paper for his English class**, he watched television.   6._____

7. **While I did my homework**, I listened to my roommate snore.   7._____

8. The career center offers seminars to anyone **who needs help writing a resume.**   8._____

9. There is much excitement **whenever election results are announced.**   9._____

10. The detective listened carefully to the suspect's answers, **but she couldn't find reason to charge the suspect.**   10._____

11. Few Americans realize **that their homes are full of minute dust mites.**   11._____

12. My first impression was **that someone had been in my room quite recently.**   12._____

13. The actress **who had lost the Oscar** declared through clenched teeth that she was delighted just to have been nominated.   13._____

14. He dropped a letter in the mailbox; **then he went to the library.**   14._____

15. The candidate decided to withdraw from the city council race **because she didn't approve of the media's treatment of her mental illness.**   15._____

16. Why don't you sit here **until the rest of the class arrives**?   16._____

17. The real estate mogul, **who is not known for his modesty**, has named still another parking lot after himself.   17._____

18. **Although he is fifty-two years old**, he is very youthful in appearance.   18._____

19. The student was excited **when she realized that she made the highest score on the chemistry exam.**   19._____

20. **Why she never smiles** is a mystery to her colleagues.   20._____

21. **Why don't you wait** until you have all the facts?   21. _____

22. She is a person **whom everyone respects and admires**.   22. _____

23. The weather is surprisingly warm **even though it is December**.   23. _____

24. My answer was **that I had been unavoidably detained**.   24. _____

25. The cat loved to sleep in the boys' room **because it could stalk their goldfish
    at night**.   25. _____

26. The trophy will be awarded to **whoever wins the contest**.   26. _____

27. The detective walked up the stairs; **he opened the door of the guest room**.   27. _____

28. Is this the book **that you asked us to order for you**?   28. _____

29. The audience could not believe **that the show would be delayed for an hour**.   29. _____

30. My Aunt Minnie Matilda, **who wrote piano duets for children**, died penniless.   30. _____

31. **Because students are prone to resolving conflicts by fighting with one another**,
    the principal is working on developing conflict resolution groups.   31. _____

32. The log cabin **where my father** was born is still standing.   32. _____

33. Many Americans realize **that dual-income families are a result of a declining
    economy rather than gender equality**.   33. _____

24. GRAMMAR: CLAUSES

(Study 24, Kinds of Dependent Clauses)

Identify the **dependent** clause in each sentence by writing its first and last words.
Then write in the number to classify it as (1) **adjective**, (2) **adverb**, or (3) **noun**.

Example: The band was dividing money when the police arrived.   ____when____ ___arrived___ _2_

1. Although most Americans want better city services, over fifty percent complain about high taxes.   1._____ _____ ____

2. The children of the war-torn city search each day for a place where the gunfire won't reach them.   2._____ _____ ____

3. The early bicycles weren't comfortable because they had wooden wheels and wooden seats.   3._____ _____ ____

4. The student who complained about the food was given another dessert.   4._____ _____ ____

5. Whether Camille dyes her hair remains a mystery.   5._____ _____ ____

6. After Jonathan had read the morning paper, he threw up his hands in despair.   6._____ _____ ____

7. While I waited for David, I was able to finish my crossword puzzle.   7._____ _____ ____

8. Professor George gave extra help to anyone who asked for it.   8._____ _____ ____

9. There is always a lot of anxiety whenever final exams are held.   9._____ _____ ____

10. The coach decided that I was not going to play that year.   10._____ _____ ____

11. Even though 91 percent of all Americans graduate from high school, America has a high illiteracy rate.   11._____ _____ ____

12. Dr. Jackson, who prides himself on his fairness, declares Burton the winner.   12._____ _____ ____

13. Because the snow continued to fall quite steadily, the party was postponed.   13._____ _____ ____

14. While Americans seem more interested in their childrens's welfare, parents are spending less time with their children.   14._____ _____ ____

15. Luis remarked that he too had trouble with calculus.   15._____ _____ ____

16. It was the only mistake that I had ever seen Henning make.   16._____ _____ ____

17. During his presentation, Nathan explained how the company could increase its profits.   17._____ _____ ____

18. Most of the audience had tears in their eyes when Juliet died.   18._____ _____ ____

19. The United States, which has the highest greenhouse emissions, also subsidizes deforestation.   19._____ _____ ____

20. The candidate told his followers that he could spend one million dollars a week on the campaign.   20._____ _____ ____

25. GRAMMAR: NOUN AND ADJECTIVE CLAUSES

(Study 24A, An Adjective and 24C, a Noun Clause)

Classify each boldface dependent clause by writing in the correct number:

Noun Clause		Adjective Clause
1. used as subject	3. used as subjective complement	5. nonrestrictive (nonessential)
2. used as direct object	4. used as object of preposition	6. restrictive(essential)

Example: That she was incompetent was clear.   _____1_____

1. **Who was the more accomplished chef** remained unresolved.   1._____

2. The programmer **who wrote the new computer game** retired at twenty.   2._____

3. I don't see how anyone could object to **what the speaker said.**   3._____

4. The lab assistant gave the disk to Joan, **whom he had helped to learn the word processing software.**   4._____

5. **What he planned for the scavenger hunt** seemed really bizarre.   5._____

6. Spend the money on **whoever needs it the most.**   6._____

7. Large classes and teacher apathy are problems **that most school districts tend to ignore.**   7._____

8. A teacher's worst fear is **that her students will hate to read.**   8._____

9. Glenn is a person **who seems to thrive on hard work and tight deadlines.**   9._____

10. Animal rights activists demonstrated in states **where grizzly bear hunting is still allowed.**   10._____

11. Samuel F. B. Morse, **who is famous for his promotion of the telegraph,** was also a successful portrait painter.   11._____

12. Children learn sexual identity by **how their parents introduce gender roles.**   12._____

13. The long, black limousine, **which had been waiting in front of the building,** sped away suddenly.   13._____

14. At the time of Columbus's voyage to America, there were over 300 Native American tribes, **which totaled more than a million people.**   14._____

15. **What you decide to do now** is critically important.   15._____

16. The author **who wrote the biography on Jane Austen** is obviously enthralled by this nineteenth-century writer.   16._____

17. The jackpot will be won by **whoever holds the lucky number.**   17._____

18. Abigail Adams, **who was America's second First Lady,** wrote a series of letters to her granddaughters.   18._____

19. Corporate spies claim **that bribing employees is the easiest way to acquire information.**   19._____

20.   The alarm sounded at the moment **that Harold was receiving his award.**   20. _____

21.   We were appalled by **what he had to tell us regarding the episode.**   21. _____

22.   **That the war was already lost** could no longer be denied.   22. _____

23.   The Black Hills is the site **where paleontologists unearthed the most complete** *Tyrannosaurus rex* **ever found.**   23. _____

24.   John's friendly demeanor is **what has helped him during tense negotiations at work.**   24. _____

25.   The Augustus Saint-Gaudens is a double eagle $20 gold piece **that was issued in the United States before 1933.**   25. _____

26. GRAMMAR: ADVERB CLAUSES

(Study 24B, An Adverb Clause)

Classify each boldface adverb clause:

1. time (when, after, until, etc.)
2. place (where, wherever)
3. manner (as, as if, as though)
4. cause (because, since)
5. purpose (that, so that, etc.)

6. condition (if, unless, etc.)
7. concession (although, though)
8. result (that)
9. degree or comparison (as, than)

Example: There would be a recount **if I had my way**.   ___6___

1.   **Because over 400,000 American get skin cancer each year**, many parents are teaching their children to avoid over-exposure to sunlight.   1._____

2.   The candidate was willing to speak **wherever she could find an audience.**   2._____

3.   Carl ran **as if his life depended on it.**   3._____

4.   She has always been able to read much faster **than her brother has.**   4._____

5.   **If I were you**, I would turn in my paper before leaving for spring break.   5._____

6.   Many trees have poisonous leaves **so that insects will not destroy them.**   6._____

7.   Most of the audience left **before the concert was half over.**   7._____

8.   I worked on the project as hard **as I could.**   8._____

9.   He read extensively **in order that he might be well prepared for the test.**   9._____

10.   **Unless American attitudes change**, small family farms will soon disappear.   10._____

11.   **Although his grades were satisfactory**, he did not qualify for the scholarship.   11._____

12.   She had worried so much **that she could no longer function effectively.**   12._____

13.   **Whether or not you accept the position**, you should write a thank-you note to the interviewer.   13._____

14.   **Because farmers were given more money for their crops**, food prices will increase significantly for consumers.   14._____

15.   She danced so hard **that she needed to rest.**   15._____

16.   Do not complete the rest of the form **until you have seen your advisor.**   16._____

17.   **Although he was only 5 feet 5 inches tall**, he was determined to be a basketball star.   17._____

18.   **Even though fax machines are convenient**, their technology increases the chance that a corporation will be victimized by corporate spies.   18._____

19.   Robert preferred to vacation **where no one stood in lines for anything.**   19._____

20.   **When the litmus paper turns red**, the substance is an acid.   20._____

21.   Andre ran so fast **that his toupee flew off his head.**   21._____

22. She usually received better grades **than her brother did.**   22. _____

23. Ethnic jokes can be particularly harmful, **since such humor subtly reinforces stereotypes.**   23. _____

24. Zoology graduates won't find jobs as zookeepers **unless they have a minor in education and experience handling animals.**   24. _____

25. She smiled **as if she knew something not known to the rest of us.**   25. _____

27. GRAMMAR: KINDS OF SENTENCE

(Study 25, Clauses in Sentences)

Classify each sentence:

A. simple   **B. compound**   **C. complex**   **D. compound/complex**

(**Any** subordinate clauses in the first ten sentences are in boldface.)

Example: He opened the throttle, and the boat sped off.   ___B___

1. Mr. Taylor still insisted **that he was an excellent driver.**   1._____

2. The comedienne, **who has a popular television series,** is starring in a movie.   2._____

3. Completion of the new library will be delayed **unless funds become available.**   3._____

4. Consider the matter carefully **before you decide**; your decision will be final.   4._____

5. This year, either medical companies or discount store chains are a good investment for the small investor.   5._____

6. The play, **which was written and produced by a colleague,** was well received by the audience.   6._____

7. The storm, **which had caused much damage,** subsided; we then continued on our hike.   7._____

8. We waited **until all the spectators had left the gymnasium.**   8._____

9. The site for the theater having been selected, construction was begun.   9._____

10. The prescription was supposed to cure my hives, instead it made my condition grow worse.   10._____

11. His career as a spy being ended, he settled in Vermont and began writing his memoirs.   11._____

12. The populations of industrialized nations are growing slowly; and therefore, the economies of these countries are on the decline.   12._____

13. His chief worry was that he might reveal the secret by talking in his sleep.   13._____

14. The television special accurately portrayed life in the 1950s; critics, therefore, praised the production for its authenticity.   14._____

15. The story appearing in the school paper contained several inaccuracies.   15._____

16. The police officer picked up the package and inspected it carefully.   16._____

17. Because she was eager to get an early start, Sue packed the night before.   17._____

18. By 2080, there will be over one million Americans 100 years or older; this significant increase of centenarians will impact the health care system.   18._____

19. Noticing the late arrivals, the speaker motioned for them to be seated.   19._____

20. A study of people in their eighties revealed that most had a satisfying relationship with a family member or care provider; in other words, these older Americans were not lonely in their old age.

20._____

21. The suspect went to the police station and turned himself in.

21._____

22. The Sierra Club will fight against any agreement that allows states to cut down ancient American forests.

22._____

23. The little girl who won the poetry contest plans to be a writer.

23._____

24. Africa has always been a major source of cultural ideas, and today modern African nations continue to export artistic and musical products.

24._____

25. The house that we wanted was sold; consequently, we had to look for another one.

25._____

26. Scientists from all over the world convened to discus the increasingly serious problem of the greenhouse effect.

26._____

27. In the 1990s, Americans are celebrating their cultural and ethnic heritage; many recent movies reflect this interest.

27._____

28. Batik—a distinctive and complex method of dying cloth—was created on the Indonesian island of Java.

28._____

29. Incredibly, Americans are paying high prices to buy software that performs simple tasks, such as balancing checkbooks.

29._____

30. Although Amy's choreography won praise opening night, she wasn't satisfied; therefore, she spent the next morning reworking it.

30._____

31. Did she appear tired?

31._____

32. A computer company recently announced a personal digital assistant, which is essentially a computerized notepad.

32._____

33. In the twentieth century, all nations have become economically dependent on each other.

33._____

34. Among wealthy nations, Japan is the only country that has a lower personal income tax than the United States.

34._____

35. The American Dream seems inaccessible to many Americans having difficulty even making ends meet.

35._____

36. Most artwork represents forms found in real life; in other words, it is the artist's job to represent familiar shapes through elements that appeal to a particular culture.

36._____

37. Couples marrying before the age of 30 experience a high divorce rate.

37._____

38. Banks promise their customers that banking will become increasingly more convenient through computer technology.

38._____

39. In our community, a Jewish vocational center has established a resettlement for Russian immigrants.

39._____

40. Women were portrayed as equals in ancient Japanese folk tales.

40._____

41. All the student organizations pledged to help fund a multicultural center, for everyone recognized the importance of developing more effective communication among the various cultural groups on campus.

41._____

42. Evan smacked his lips and plowed through another stack of buttermilk pancakes smothered in blueberry syrup.

42._____

43. In Texas, we grew to love that white gravy served on chicken-fried steak.

43._____

44. Because of his ruddy complexion, David had to endure the nickname of Pinky when he was a little boy.

44. _____

45. The Middle East was the birthplace of three major world religions—Judaism, Christianity, and Islam.

45. _____

46. The women sat up late one night talking about their first dates; most laughed about their awkward teenage years.

46. _____

47. Most theorists describe reading as an interactive process between the reader and the text.

47. _____

48. When Holly Jo stepped into my office and hollered her familiar, "Y'all," I knew that I was about to be treated to a juicy bit of gossip.

48. _____

49. Animal crackers were originally designed as a Christmas treat.

49. _____

50. The three favorite amusements in the 1920s were mahjong, ouija, and crossword puzzles.

50. _____

28. GRAMMAR: AGREEMENT—SUBJECT AND VERB

(Study 26, Make Every Verb Agree with Its Subject in Person)

Write the number of the **correct** choice.

Example: One of my favorite programs (1)**was** (2)**were** canceled. _____1_____

1. Neither the researcher nor the subject (1)**has** (2)**have** any idea which is the placebo. 1. _____

2. Economics (1)**is** (2)**are** what the students are most interested in. 2. _____

3. Working a second job to pay off my debts (1)**has** (2)**have** become a priority. 3. _____

4. Not one of the nominees (1)**has** (2)**have** impressed me. 4. _____

5. (1)**Does** (2)**Do** each of the questions count the same number of points? 5. _____

6. The number of jobs lost in California's Silicon Valley (1)**has** (2)**have** increased significantly in the past two years. 6. _____

7. Ninety-nine (1)**is** (2)**are** hyphenated because it is a compound number. 7. _____

8. The college president, along with five vice presidents, (1)**was** (2)**were** ready for the meeting. 8. _____

9. Both the secretary and the treasurer (1)**was** (2)**were** asked to submit reports. 9. _____

10. Everyone in the audience (1)**was** (2)**were** surprised by the mayor's remarks. 10. _____

11. Women (1)**is** (2)**are** a common noun, plural in number. 11. _____

12. Every junior and senior (1)**was** (2)**were** expected to report to the gymnasium. 12. _____

13. There (1)**is** (2)**are** a professor, several students, and a teaching assistant meeting to discuss the course reading list. 13. _____

14. Ten dollars (1)**is** (2)**are** too much to pay for that book. 14. _____

15. (1)**Is** (2)**Are** there any computers available in the lab this morning? 15. _____

16. Neither the neighbors nor the police officer (1)**was** (2)**were** surprised by the violent crime. 16. _____

17. Each of the crises actually (1)**needs** (2)**need** the President's immediate attention. 17. _____

18. (1)**Is** (2)**Are** your father and brother coming to see you graduate tomorrow? 18. _____

19. A good book and some chocolate donuts (1)**was** (2)**were** all she needed to relax. 19. _____

20. There (1)**is** (2)**are** one coat and two hats in the hallway. 20. _____

21. (1)**Does** (2)**Do** Coach Jasek and the players know about the special award? 21. _____

22. My two weeks' vacation (1)**was** (2)**were** filled with many projects around the house. 22. _____

23. The only thing that annoyed me more (1)**was** (2)**were** the children tracking mud in from the backyard. 23. _____

24. (1)**Hasn't** (2)**Haven't** either of the roommates looked for the missing ring? 24. _____

25. There (1)**is** (2)**are** one bird and two squirrels fighting over the birdseed in the feeder.

25. _____

26. On the table (1)**was** (2)**were** a pen, a pad of paper, and two rulers.

26. _____

27. It's remarkable that the entire class (1)**is** (2)**are** passing this summer.

27. _____

28. It (1)**was** (2)**were** a book and a disk that disappeared from the desk.

28. _____

29. There (1)**is** (2)**are** many opportunities for part-time employment on campus.

29. _____

30. (1)**Is** (2)**Are** algebra and chemistry required courses?

30. _____

31. One of his three instructors (1)**has**(2)**have** offered to write a letter of recommendation.

31. _____

32. (1)**Does** (2)**Do** either of the books have a section on usage rules?

32. _____

33. Neither my parents' car nor our own old jeep (1)**is** (2)**are** reliable enough to make the trip.

33. _____

34. Marbles, stones, and string (1)**is** (2)**are** my son's favorite playthings.

34. _____

35. Each of the books (1)**has** (2)**have** an introduction written by the author's mentor.

35. _____

36. The lab report, in addition to several short papers, (1)**was** (2)**were** due immediately after spring break.

36. _____

37. Neither the teacher nor the parents (1)**understands** (2)**understand** why Nathan does so well in math but can barely read first-grade books.

37. _____

38. The old woman who walks the twin Scottish terriers (1)**detests** (2)**detest** small children running on the sidewalk in front of her house.

38. _____

39. At the Boy Scout camp out, eggs and bacon (1)**was** (2)**were** the first meal the troop attempted to prepare on an open fire.

39. _____

40. There (1)**is**(2)**are** language, social relations, interests, and geographical origins to help define cultural groups.

40. _____

41. Everyone (1)**was**(2)**were** working hard to finish planting the crops before the rainy season.

41. _____

42. The children, along with their teacher, (1)**is** (2)**are** preparing a one-act play for the spring open house.

42. _____

43. Minnie Olson is one of those people who always (1)**volunteers** (2)**volunteer** to help the homeless.

43. _____

44. Lucy announced that *The Holy Terrors* (1)**is** (2)**are** the title of her next book, which is about raising her three sons.

44. _____

45. The class, along with the teacher, (1)**was** (2)**were** worried about the ailing class pet.

45. _____

46. Five dollars (1)**does** (2)**do** not seem like much to my eight-year-old son.

46. _____

47. Either the choir members or the organist (1)**was** (2)**were** constantly battling with the minister about purchasing fancy new choir robes.

47. _____

48. In the last 200 years, over 50 million people from 140 countries (1)**has** (2)**have** left their homelands to immigrate to the United States.

48. _____

49. Food from different geographic locations and ethnic groups often (1)**helps** (2)**help** distinguish specific cultural events.

49. _____

50. Because Mercury is hard to see, not much (1)**was** (2)**were** known about this planet until the 1960s and 1970s.

50. _____

29. GRAMMAR: AGREEMENT—SUBJECT AND VERB

(Study 26, Make Every Verb Agree with Its Subject in Person and Number)

Write the number of the **correct** choice.

Example: Neither Sarah nor her parents (1)**was** (2)**were** ready to leave the fairgrounds.   ___2___

1. Virtually every painting and every sculpture Picasso did (1)**is** (2)**are** worth over a million dollars.   1._____

2. There on the table (1)**was** (2)**were** my wallet and my key chain.   2._____

3. Neither the documentary about beekeeping nor the two shows about Iceland (1)**was** (2)**were** successful in the ratings.   3._____

4. Each of the new television series (1)**is** (2)**are** about single-parent families.   4._____

5. Sitting on the sidewalk (1)**was** (2)**were** Amy and her four best friends.   5._____

6. *Les Atrides* (1)**is** (2)**are** a ten-hour, four-play production of ancient Greek theater.   6._____

7. A political convention, with its candidates, delegates and reporters, (1)**seems** (2)**seem** like bedlam.   7._____

8. In the auditorium (1)**was** (2)**were** assembled the orchestra members who were ready to practice for the upcoming concert.   8._____

9. Each of the art historians (1)**has** (2)**have** offered a theory for why the Leonardo painting has such a stark background.   9._____

10. (1)**Was** (2)**Were** either President Smith or Dean Nicholson asked to speak at the awards ceremony?   10._____

11. Watching local high school basketball games (1)**has** (2)**have** become his favorite weekend activity.   11._____

12. His baseball and his glove (1)**was** (2)**were** all Jamil was permitted to take to the game.   12._____

13. Neither my friends nor I (1)**expects** (2)**expect** to go on the overnight trip.   13._____

14. My coach and mentor (1)**is** (2)**are** Gwen Johnson.   14._____

15. *Vanity Fair*, along with *The New Yorker,* (1)**has** (2)**have** had a woman editor.   15._____

16. The researcher, as well as her assistants, (1)**is** (2)**are** developing a study to compare the brain tissue of Alzheimer sufferers and healthy subjects.   16._____

17. Neither criticism nor frequent failures (1)**was** (2)**were** enough to retard his progress.   17._____

18. Where (1)**is** (2)**are** the end of the recession and the beginning of economic recovery?   18._____

19. She is the only one of six candidates who (1)**refuses** (2)**refuse** to speak at the ceremony.   19._____

20. Neither the systems analyst nor the accountants (1)**was** (2)**were** able to locate the problem in the computer program.   20._____

21. Economics (1)**has** (2)**have** been the most dismal science I've ever studied. 21. _____

22. (1)**Has** (2)**Have** either of your letters appeared in the newspaper? 22. _____

23. It (1)**was** (2)**were** the general and the secretary of state who finally convinced the President that an armed conflict might be inevitable. 23. _____

24. Neither Janet nor her parents (1)**seems** (2)**seem** interested in our offer to help. 24. _____

25. He is one of those employees who (1)**was** (2)**were** always late for work on Monday mornings. 25. _____

30. GRAMMAR: AGREEMENT—PRONOUN AND ANTECEDENT

(Study 27, Make Every Pronoun Agree with Its Antecedent in Person and Number)

Write in the number of the **correct** choice.

Example: One of the riders fell off (1)**his** (2)**their** horse. _____1_____

1. Agatha Christie is the kind of writer who loves to keep (1)**her** (2)**their** readers guessing until the last page. 1._____

2. Many tourists traveling in the West enjoy stopping at roadside attractions because (1)**we** (2)**they** never know what to expect. 2._____

3. If anyone has found my wallet, will (1)**he or she** (2)**you** please return it. 3._____

4. He majored in mathematics because (1)**it** (2)**they** had always been of interest to him. 4._____

5. Lucy edited the news because (1)**it was** (2)**they** was often full of inaccuracies. 5._____

6. He assumed that all of his students had done (1)**his** (2)**their** best to complete the test. 6._____

7. Both Ed and Luis decided to stretch (1)**his or her** (2)**their** legs when the bus reached Houston. 7._____

8. Ironically, neither woman had considered how to make (1)**her** (2)**their** job easier. 8._____

9. Each of the researchers spent several hours explaining (1)**his or her** (2)**(remove the pronoun)** theories about the age of the solar system. 9._____

10. He buys his books at the campus bookstore because (1)**it has** (2)**they have** low prices. 10._____

11. Neither the president nor the members of the community advisory committee were willing to ignore (1)**her** (2)**their** personal opinions to find a solution to the city's budgetary problems. 11._____

12. Every member of the men's basketball team received (1)**his** (2)**their** individual trophy. 12._____

13. The class voted to have (1)**its** (2)**their** term papers due a week earlier. 13._____

14. The jury seemed to be having difficulty in making up (1)**its mind** (2)**their minds**. 14._____

15. Neither Aaron nor Marzell has declared (1)**his** (2)**their** major. 15._____

16. Citizens who still do not recycle (1)**your** (2)**their** garbage need to read this news article. 16._____

17. Before someone can choose a career rationally, (1)**he or she** (2)**they** must have sufficient information. 17._____

18. Neither the guide nor the hikers seemed aware of (1)**her** (2)**their** danger on the trail. 18._____

19. The faculty has already selected (1)**its** (2)**their** final candidates. 19._____

20. Critics argue that (1)**those kind** (2)**those kinds** of movies may promote violent tendencies in children.   20._____

21. One has to decide early in life what (1)**he or she** (2)**they** want out of life.   21._____

22. Neither the coach nor the players underestimated (1)**his or her** (2)**their** opponents.   22._____

23. Roy Rogers and Dale Evans were known as the King and Queen of the West by (1)**his or her** (2)**their** adoring fans from the 1940s.   23._____

24. Students should take accurate and complete notes so that (1)**they** (2)**you** will be prepared for the exam.   24._____

25. Neither the team nor the coach is happy about (1)**her** (2)**their** budget for the coming school year.   25._____

26. In the next five years, owners of older vehicles polluting the environment can sell (1)**their** (2)**your** cars or trucks for scrap.   26._____

27. If a stranger tried to talk to her, she would just look at (1)**him** (2)**them** and smile.   27._____

28. Every one of the trees in the affected area had lost most of (1)**its** (2)**their** leaves.   28._____

29. Some women can understand (1)**herself** (2)**themself** (3)**themselves** better through reading feminist literature.   29._____

30. The medical committee was surprised to learn that (1)**its** (2)**their** preliminary findings had been published in the newspaper.   30._____

31. The campus disciplinary board determined that (1)**its** (2)**their** process for reviewing student complaints was too cumbersome and slow.   31._____

32. No one should blame (1)**himself** (2)**themself** (3)**themselves** (4)**yourself** for misfortunes that cannot be prevented.   32._____

33. Rita is a person who cannot control (1)**her** (2)**their** anger when under stress.   33._____

34. Professor Brown is one of those teachers who really love (1)**his** (2)**their** profession.   34._____

35. Everyone grabbed (1)**his** (2)**their** boots and gloves when the heavy snowstorm hit the campus.   35._____

36. Neither the peer counselors nor the dorm director looked forward to how (1)**their** (2)**her** residents would react to the rodent population that had invaded the building.   36._____

37. Each of the singers in the newly formed Irish band dreamed of earning (1)**her** (2)**their** first million dollars.   37._____

38. As part of the Kim family's Vietnamese New Year celebration, each wrote *cau doi*— which are poems about (1)**his or her** (2)**their** memories of home and family.   38._____

39. During the Christmas season, many Latin American families serve (1)**its** (2)**their** favorite dish—tortillas spread with mashed avocado and roast chicken.   39._____

40. If everyone would contribute a small portion of (1)**her** (2)**their** January 1 paycheck, we should be able to purchase the microwave for the staff luncheon room.   40._____

41. Each cat claimed (1)**its** (2)**their** specific area of the bedroom for long afternoon naps.   41._____

42. The hearing impaired now have a telecommunication device to allow (1)**he** (2)**them** to make phone calls to a hearing person.   42._____

43. When my professors complain that Americans don't support local school districts, I remind (1)**her** (2)**them** that most families view education as extremely important.   43._____

44. Everyone came to the last class to make certain (1)**he or she** (2)**they** understood the professor's requirements for the final.

44. _____

45. If viewers are not happy with public television programming, (1)**you** (2)**they** should write letters to local television stations.

45. _____

46. Researchers have found that the type of relationship couples have can affect (1)**your** (2)**their** overall immune system.

46. _____

47. Neither the computer assistants nor the hardware specialist knows how (1)**she or he** (2)**they** should solve the current printer problem.

47. _____

48. The researchers stated that (1)**she doesn't** (2)**they don't really** understand the psychological ramifications of obesity.

48. _____

49. A neighborhood organization of young people is meeting to determine how (1)**it** (2)**they** can help elderly neighbors in the community.

49. _____

50. Either the lead actor or the chorus members missed (1)**his** (2)**their** cue.

50. _____

31. GRAMMAR: AGREEMENT—REVIEW

(Study 26-27, Agreement)

Write 1 if the sentence is **correct** in agreement. Write 0 if it is **incorrect**.

Example: Nobody in the first two rows are singing. _____0_____

1. The deep blue of the waters seem to reflect the sky. 1._____

2. At the highlight of the Passover holiday, all of the family participates in the Seder, which is a ceremonial feast. 2._____

3. Joe's passion is fast cars. 3._____

4. The strength of these new space-age materials have been demonstrated many times. 4._____

5. All these experiences, along with the special love and care that my daughter needs, have taught me the value of caring. 5._____

6. Evan's pants are ripped beyond repair. 6._____

7. Does the six-thirty bus and the eight-o'clock train arrive in Detroit before midnight? 7._____

8. According to a recent survey, almost every American feels that their self-esteem is important. 8._____

9. The management now realizes that a bigger budget is needed; they plan to ask for federal assistance. 9._____

10. When an older student senses that an institution understands nontraditional students, she generally works to her academic potential. 10._____

11. I found that the thrill of attending college soon leaves when you have to visit the bursar's office. 11._____

12. Everyone who read the letter stated that they were surprised by the contents. 12._____

13. You should hire one of those experts who solves problems with computers. 13._____

14. Two hundred miles was too much for a day trip. 14._____

15. At school, there are constant noise and confusion at lunch. 15._____

16. Cleveland or Cincinnati are planning to host the statewide contests. 16._____

17. Bacon and eggs are no longer considered a healthy breakfast. 17._____

18. Probably everybody in the computer center, except Colleen and Aaron, know how to run the scanner. 18._____

19. Neither Chuck nor Arnold are as blessed with talent as Sylvester. 19._____

20. *The Avengers* was a popular British television show in the 1960s. 20._____

32. GRAMMAR: FRAGMENTS

(Study 29A, Fragments)

Write **1** if the boldface words are a **complete sentence**.
Write **0** if they are a **fragment**.

Example: Luis was famished. **Having eaten only four hot dogs at the game.** _____ 0

1. **When interviewing applicants for the nanny position.** It's important to review all references.

2. **Having applied for dozens of jobs and not having had any offers.**

3. **The manuscript having been returned, Johanna sat down to revise it.**

4. Harrison desperately wanted the part. **Because he believed that this was the film that would make him a star.**

5. The exercise bike was dusty. **Sue never seemed to have time to use it.**

6. He admitted to being a computer nerd. **As a matter of fact, he was proud of his computing skills.**

7. **Over 50 percent of Americans surveyed feel guilty about their child-care arrangements.**

8. I read all of the articles. **Then I wrote the first draft of my paper.**

9. Many Americans prefer indirect business levies rather than direct taxation. **Where do you stand on this issue?**

10. Maurice kept nodding his head as the coach explained the play. **Thinking all the time that it would never work.**

11. **Because she was interested in rocks, she majored in geology.**

12. I argued with two of my classmates. **First with Edward and then with Harry.**

13. There are many humorous research projects. **Such as developing an artificial dog to breed fleas for allergy studies.**

14. Taylor was absolutely positive he would pass. **Regardless of having received failing grades on both his essay and the mid-term.**

15. **Colleen stepped up to the free-throw line; then she made two points to win the game.**

16. **His term paper having been returned.** He looked eagerly for the instructor's grade.

17. **Because he never really examined the contract.**

18. She went to the supermarket. **After she had made a list of groceries that she needed.**

19. **Two days before the competition, he felt nervous.** However, right before the contest, he felt very confident.

1. _____
2. _____
3. _____
4. _____
5. _____
6. _____
7. _____
8. _____
9. _____
10. _____
11. _____
12. _____
13. _____
14. _____
15. _____
16. _____
17. _____
18. _____
19. _____

20. I telephoned Dr. Gross. **The man who had been our family physician for many years.**

20. _____

21. We suspect Harry of the theft. **Because he had access to the funds and he has been living far beyond his means.**

21. _____

22. Perhaps we should pay close attention to the candidate's position on education. **Especially since the families are unhappy with the local school district.**

22. _____

23. Please don't go. **Stay.**

23. _____

24. She is a star athlete. **Beside being a brilliant student.**

24. _____

25. I offered her a ticket to *Mousetrap.* **A play she had wanted to see.**

25. _____

26. The winter weather was brutal this year because of the heavy snowfall. **About ten feet in total.**

26. _____

27. **Knowing that her time was limited, she took a taxi to the station.**

27. _____

28. **To prevent further damage to the sun room roof.** We decided to hire someone to remove the snow and ice.

28. _____

29. Successful Presidents in the past twenty-five years have learned. **To avoid overexposure in the media.**

29. _____

30. Roger Maris never received the credit he deserved. **Despite breaking Babe Ruth's record for home runs in a single season.**

30. _____

31. **Although settlers began coming to America in the sixteenth century.** It wasn't until the nineteenth century that large groups of Europeans came to this country.

31. _____

32. **While many African-Americans commemorate their African ancestors and traditional community values during Kwanza.**

32. _____

33. **Listen!** It's too hot to do much yard work today without taking frequent rests in the shade.

33. _____

33. GRAMMAR: COMMA SPLICES AND FUSED SENTENCES

(Study 29B, Comma Splices and Fused Sentences)

Write 1 for each item that is a **single complete sentence**.
Write 0 for each item that is a **comma splice** or **fused sentence**.

Example: The mission was a success, everyone was pleased.   ___0___

1.   The critics unanimously agreed the play was terrible it closed after a week.   1._____

2.   The party broke up at one in the morning, Jack lingered for a few final words
     with Kathy.   2._____

3.   Determined to sweep the southern and western states, the President authorized
     extra campaign money to be spent there.   3._____

4.   If the moon enters the earth's shadow, a lunar eclipse occurs, causing the moon to
     turn a deep red.   4._____

5.   The ticket agent had sold eighty-one tickets to boarding passengers, yet there were
     only eleven empty seats on the train.   5._____

6.   Since she was in the mood for a romantic movie, she hired a babysitter and went to
     see the movie *Sense and Sensibility.*   6._____

7.   Sheer exhaustion having caught up with me, I had no trouble falling asleep.   7._____

8.   The restaurant check almost made me faint, because I had left my wallet home,
     I couldn't pay for the meal.   8._____

9.   Those of us who lived in off-campus housing ignored the rule, since we were seniors,
     we never worried about campus regulations.   9._____

10. It was a cloudy, sultry afternoon when we sighted our first school of whales, and
     the cry of "Lower the boats!" rang throughout the ship.   10._____

11. The war was finally over; however, little could be done to ease the refugees' sense
     of loss.   11._____

12. The author described fifty ways to recycle fruitcakes; my favorite is to use slices of
     fruitcake as drink coasters.   12._____

13. The three major television networks face stiff competition for ratings, because of
     cable networks, viewers can decide from over four hundred programs.   13._____

14. The doctor recommended that we eliminate excessive sugar from our diet, I now
     read all product labels.   14._____

15. While the teacher believed that it was important for her students to write everyday,
     she didn't enjoy grading so many papers.   15._____

16. Americans earn less than they did ten years ago; skyrocketing health care costs are
     often cited as the leading cause for the decline in income.   16._____

17. Crime is still a major concern for many Americans because so many teenagers
     are arrested for violent crimes.   17._____

18. As I waited in line for my turn at the automatic teller machine, I balanced my checkbook.

18._____

19. Over 30 percent of children from rural American live in mobile homes, therefore, Congress has established a commission to study mobile home safety and construction standards.

19._____

20. A shortage of licensed contractors often exists in the areas hit by natural disasters, yet homeowners quickly learn to wait for a work crew with the proper credentials.

20._____

21. The largest Native American reservation is the Navajo it is located mostly in Arizona and covers 16 million acres.

21._____

22. According to some researchers, little boys may have different educational experiences from little girls, in other words, even though it may be unintentional, teachers often have subtly different expectations based on the gender of their students.

22._____

23. Tarantulas, which are large spiders with powerful fangs and a mean bite, live not only in the tropics but also in the United States.

23._____

24. Polygraph evidence in criminal cases may not be used in a trial unless both the prosecution and the defense lawyers agree before any lie detector test is given.

24._____

25. The software game was full of violent scenes, therefore, it was banned from the school's computer center.

25._____

34. GRAMMAR: FRAGMENTS, COMMA SPLICES, AND FUSED SENTENCES

(Study 29A, Fragments, and 29B, Comma Splices and Fused Sentences)

Write 1 for each item that is a **single complete sentence**.
Write 0 for each item that is a **fragment**.

Example: A man who neither seeks out trouble nor avoids it.   ___0___

1. Because pie, ice cream, and candy bars have practically no nutritional value.   1. _____

2. When the bindings release, the ski comes off.   2. _____

3. Which promotes tooth decay when not used properly   3. _____

4. Lady Bird Johnson and Eleanor Roosevelt, First Ladies greatly admired.   4. _____

5. Whereas older cars run on regular gas and lack complex pollution controls.   5. _____

6. That particular judicial hearing raised issues of how men and women perceive
    each other.   6. _____

7. By installing smoke detectors, families may someday save family members from
    perishing in a fire.   7. _____

8. Watching from the seventh floor during the parade.   8. _____

9. Which could strengthen your immune system.   9. _____

10. Stay.   10. _____

Write **1** for each item that is **one or more complete, correct sentences**.
Write **2** for each item that contains a **fragment**.
Write **3** for each item that contains a **comma splice** or **fused sentence**.

Example: Today is Monday, tomorrow is Tuesday.   ___3___

1. We planned the trip carefully yet we still had a series of disasters.   1. _____

2. The quarterback signed the largest professional sports contract to date; he will
    earn $43 million over a six-year period.   2. _____

3. Native Americans have dances and music for every tribal ceremony and social
    occasion celebrated.   3. _____

4. Scientists are currently interested in studying polar bears. Because the bears' body
    chemistry may reveal how pollution has affected the Arctic.   4. _____

5. Americans, for the moment, may be less concerned about taxes. Polls indicate that
    Americans would rather balance the federal budget than lower taxes.   5. _____

6. The applicant squirmed in her chair because she was not prepared for the
    interviewer's questions.   6. _____

7. The community was unaware of the city's plan to tear down a playground, therefore, few citizens attended the city council meetings.

7. _____

8. Since 1975, over 1.5 million Vietnamese have left their homeland in search of a peaceful life, many have settled in Australia, Canada, Europe, and the United States.

8. _____

9. Because the founder of a popular fast-food restaurant chain has encouraged corporations to provide financial support for employees adopting children.

9. _____

10. All my co-workers are on diets and won't eat any cookies or cake.

10. _____

11. What happened to Clyde, Roberta, and Sondra is told in the novel *An American Tragedy* it was written by Theodore Dreiser.

11. _____

12. He wore a pair of mud-encrusted, flap-soled boots they looked older than he was.

12. _____

13. He wore a pair of mud-encrusted, flap-soled boots, footgear that looked older than he was.

13. _____

14. The computer analyst produced pages of statistics, for the agency wanted to know how its money was spent.

14. _____

15. Enrique reread his assignment a dozen times before handing it in. To be absolutely sure his ideas were clear.

15. _____

16. The executive waited, however, until every worker at the meeting presented his or her point of view.

16. _____

17. That she is dead is beyond dispute.

17. _____

18. "I believe," declared the headmaster. "That you deserve expulsion."

18. _____

19. The scouts hiked two miles until they reached the falls, then they had lunch.

19. _____

20. The police having been warned to expect trouble, every available officer lined the avenue of the march.

20. _____

21. A still greater challenge faced the firefighters, it seemed impossible to build the fire wall in time to protect a cluster of houses at the edge of the forest.

21. _____

22. In the 1800s, Ireland's vital crop was wiped out by the potato blight, nevertheless, Irish people who owned ten acres of land were disqualified from poor relief.

22. _____

23. The Irish immigrants did not settle on farms for fear that the potato blight would strike again, but the German immigrants did go into farming, they had no fear of this blight.

23. _____

35. GRAMMAR: SENTENCE EFFECTIVENESS

(Study 28-29, Effective Sentences)

For each **correct** sentence, write **1**.
For each **incorrect** (ineffective) sentence, write the number that **explains** the error:
  2. **failure to subordinate details**
  3. **childishly choppy sentences**
  4. **overuse of** *and*
  5. **needless separation of subject and verb or parts of infinitive**
  6. **dangling, misplaced, or squinting modifier**
  7. **nonparallel structure**
  8. **incomplete comparisons or expressions of degree**
  9. **shift in person, number, tense, voice, etc.**
  10. **redundancy (including double negative and superfluous** *that*)
  11. **mixed construction**
  12. **inflated phrasing**

Example: He wanted **to shower** and **to sleep**.   ____1____

Example: That was a **most unique** moment.   ____10____

1.   If **one** drives a car without thinking, **you** are more than likely to have an accident.   1._____

2.   She said **that**, if I helped her with her math, **that** she would type my paper.   2._____

3.   The entire class was **so** pleased at learning that Dr. Turner has rescheduled the quiz.   3._____

4.   John planned to **carefully and thoughtfully** ask Julia to marry him.   4._____

5.   A study revealed that vigorous exercise may add only one or two years to a person's life. **This study used Harvard graduates**.   5._____

6.   The film director, thinking **only** about how he could get the shot of the erupting volcano, endangered everyone.   6._____

7.   With her new auditory implant, Audrey heard **so** much better.   7._____

8.   **Watching the star hitter blast a home run over the fence**, the ball smashed a windshield of an expensive sports car.   8._____

9.   The owner of the team seems **to insult her players and fans and mismanaging the finances**.   9._____

10. The witness **walked** into the courtroom, and then she **wishes** she could avoid testifying.   10._____

11. **An increase in energy taxes** causes most people to consider carpooling and improving energy conservation practices in their home.   11._____

12. According to historians, settlers traveling westward used prairie schooners, not Conestoga wagons, **and** they used oxen and mules instead of horses to pull the wagons, **and** they didn't pull their wagons in a circle when under an attack.   12._____

13. He told me **that he was going to write a letter and not to disturb him**.   13._____

14. **Ajay Smith is a senior**, and he just won national recognition for his poetry.   14._____

15. In the 1400s, many English villages held football competitions: **an inflated animal bladder was kicked or shoved between two distant points by opposing teams.** 15._____

16. If a **student** knows how to study, **he** should achieve success. 16._____

17. **He went to his office. He sat down. He opened his briefcase. He read some papers.** 17._____

18. Summer is a time for **parties, friendships, for sports,** and **in which we can relax.** 18._____

19. Juliet and I must make a decision, **within one passage of the sun across the heavens, as to whether we should be forever united in holy wedlock.** 19._____

20. The neighborhood children, **happy about school being closed because of a severe snowstorm and blowing winds,** planned an afternoon sledding party. 20._____

21. I met the new dorm counselor **in my oldest pajamas.** 21._____

22. Being a ski jumper requires nerves of steel, **you have to concentrate to the utmost, and being perfectly coordinated.** 22._____

23. **The situation in regard to decisions on the possible expenditure of my monetary resources is such that any commitment on my part to such expenditure must be considered with extreme caution.** 23._____

24. The plane neither had **enough fuel** nor **proper radar equipment.** 24._____

25. **My personal opinion is that I think** that the Athletics will win their division by ten games. 25._____

26. Students need to develop a network of friends on campus, so that **you can form study groups to work on papers and projects.** 26._____

27. He **couldn't hardly** make himself heard because of the noise outside. 27._____

28. The instructor wondered **when did the students began sneaking out of class.** 28._____

Write the number of the most effective way of expressing the given ideas.

Example:

1. At this moment in time, I regret that it was impossible for me to partake in my morning repast.

2. I had to miss breakfast.

3. I had not hardly enough time for breakfast.

    _____2_____

1. 1. There was a company in Minneapolis. It shortened its work week from 40 hours to 36 hours. The company's output increased.

2. A company in Minneapolis shortened its work week from 40 hours to 36 hours, and this company found out the company's output increased.

3. When a Minneapolis company shortened its work week from 40 to 36 hours, its output increased.

    1._____

2. 1. Broadway has been revived by a new band of actors. These new actors are from Hollywood. They find it refreshing and challenging to perform before a live audience.

    2. Broadway has been revived by a new breed of actors—Hollywood stars, who find it refreshing and challenging to perform before a live audience.

    3. Broadway has been revived by this new breed of actors, which has seen actors coming from Hollywood; they have found it refreshing and challenging to perform before a live audience.

2. _____

3. 1. Recreational tree climbing has become popular. Ecologists hope that a code of tree-climbing ethics will be developed. Such a code may help to prevent damage to the delicate forest ecosystems.

    2. Recreational tree climbing has become popular and ecologists hope that a code of tree-climbing ethics will be developed, and such a code may help to prevent damage to the delicate forest ecosystems.

    3. Before recreational tree climbing becomes any more popular, ecologists hope that a code of tree-climbing ethics will be developed to prevent permanent damage to delicate forest ecosystems.

3. _____

4. 1. Harry Truman, who woke up in the morning to find himself elected President, had gone to bed early on election night.

    2. Harry Truman, who had gone to bed early on election night, woke up the next morning to find himself elected President.

    3. Harry Truman went to bed early on election night, and he woke up the next morning and found himself elected President.

4. _____

5. 1. The papers were marked Top Secret. The term *Top Secret* indicates contents of extraordinary value.

    2. The papers were of extraordinary value, and, therefore they were marked Top Secret.

    3. The papers were market Top Secret, indicating their extraordinary value.

5. _____

36. GRAMMAR: PARALLEL STRUCTURE

(Study 28F, Use Parallel Structure)

Write **1** if the boldface words or word groups are all in **parallel structure**.
Write **0** if the boldface words or word groups are not all in **parallel structure**.

Example: Lilliputian politicians practiced **leaping** and **creeping**. ___1___

1. Charlene impressed everyone with her **wit, charm, grace, and intelligence.** 1._____

2. Before 8 a.m., my youngest son had **made himself breakfast, made a snow fort in the front yard, and tormented his brothers.** 2._____

3. The apartment could be rented **by the week, by the month, or you could pay on a yearly basis.** 3._____

4. **What I saw, what I did, and what I said** made an impression on my supervisor. 4._____

5. Our new wood-burning stove **should keep us warm, save us money, and should afford us much pleasure.** 5._____

6. Christopher Columbus has been remembered as **an entrepreneur, an explorer, a sailor, and perhaps now for how he took advantage of native populations.** 6._____

7. My grandmother's cookbook **is old, worn, and has been used by three generations of Replogle women.** 7._____

8. The chief ordered Agent 007 **to break into the building, crack the safe, and to steal the atomic yo-yo plans.** 8._____

9. A good batter knows how to **hit to the opposite field and staring down the pitcher.** 9._____

10. When kindergartners were asked how the President should behave, they said someone who was **fair, who shares,** and **not a hitter.** 10._____

Instructions: Write **1** if the sentence contains **parallel structure**.
Write **0** if the sentence is **not parallel.**

Example: The candidate took lessons in how to kiss babies and looking honest. ___0___

1. Where we go on vacation and what we do while on our trip are always decided by the entire family. 1._____

2. I knew what I was supposed to do but not when I was supposed to do it or how I could accomplish it. 2._____

3. The scouts marched briskly off into the woods, trekked ten miles to Alder Lake, and tents were erected by them. 3._____

4. Dean has three main strengths: his ability to listen, he likes people, and his interest in cultural awareness. 4._____

5. Grizzly bears have returned to ancestral behaviors both in eating and mating. 5._____

6. Global warming may not only increase air and ocean temperatures but also to strengthen the forces causing storms.

6. _____

7. The advertising copywriter realized that she had to create more impressive-sounding labels or face an angry client.

7. _____

8. Neither regulating prices nor wages will slow inflation enough.

8. _____

9. During its early years, Sears, Roebuck and Company sold not only clothes, furniture and hardware, but also customers could buy cars and houses.

9. _____

10. Charlie practiced shooting from the top of the key as well as how to dribble with either hand.

10. _____

37. GRAMMAR: PARALLEL STRUCTURE

(Study 28F, Use Parallel Structure.)

Write **1** if the boldface words or word groups are **all in parallel structure;** write **0** if they are not. Then, identify each element as follows:

2. noun (including gerunds) (with or without modifiers)
3. participle (or participial phrases)
4. verb (with or without modifiers or complement)
5. prepositional phrase
6. infinitive (or infinitive phrase)
7. clause
8. adjective

	Parallel	#1	#2	#3
Example: Grandmother insisted on **cleanliness, godliness, and being prompt.**	0	2	2	4

1.   The job required some knowledge of **word processing, desktop publishing, and to write.**
1. ____ ___ ___ ___

2.   Hector fought with **great skill, epic daring, and superb intelligence.**
2. ____ ___ ___ ___

3.   The mosques of ancient Islamic Spain typically contained **ornate stone screens, long hallways, and the columns looked like spindles.**
3. ____ ___ ___ ___

4.   The castle, **built on a hill, surrounded by farmland, and commanding a magnificent view,** protected the peasants from **invasions by hostile forces.**
4. ____ ___ ___ ___

5.   A newly discovered primate from the Amazon has **wide-set eyes, a broad nose, and the fur is striped like a zebra.**
5. ____ ___ ___ ___

6.   By nightfall, we were **tired, hungry, and grumpy.**
6. ____ ___ ___ ___

7.   The guerrillas **surrounded the village, set up their mortars, and the shelling began.**
7. ____ ___ ___ ___

8.   Kiesha did not know **where she had come from, why she was there, or the time of her departure.**
8. ____ ___ ___ ___

9.   Her favorite pastimes remain **designing clothes, cooking gourmet meals, and practicing the flute.**
9. ____ ___ ___ ___

10.   Eliot's poetry is **witty, complex, and draws on his vast learning.**
10. ____ ___ ___ ___

38. GRAMMAR: PLACEMENT OF MODIFIERS

(Study 29C, Needless Separation of Related Parts of a Sentence.)

Write **1** if the boldface word(s) are **correctly** placed.
Write **0** if the boldface word(s) are **incorrectly** placed.

Example: Never give a toy to a child **which can be swallowed.**   ___0___

1.   He ordered a pizza for his friends **covered with pepperoni.**   1._____

2.   She had enough money to by **only** two of the three books that she needed.   2._____

3.   Americans **who consider medical treatment everyone's right** are demanding a
     national health care program.   3._____

4.   After asking a few questions, we decided **to end the conference call quickly**
     because we weren't interested in what the company had to offer.   4._____

5.   We saw the plane taxi onto the field **that would soon be leaving for Chicago.** 5._____

6.   Unfortunately, many Americans are spending **almost** a third of their income on rent.   6._____

7.   Derek found a clue in his bedroom **that he had never seen before.**   7._____

8.   Unfortunately, the resale shop was full of **wrinkled** little girls' dresses.   8._____

9.   We hurriedly bought a picnic table from a clerk **with collapsible legs.**   9._____

10. We learned that no one could discard anything at the municipal dump **except
     people living in the community.**   10._____

11. The only baseball jacket left was a **green and white** child's starter jacket.   11._____

12. The race car driver planned **after her last race** to retire before she received
     another injury.   12._____

13. The bride walked down the aisle with her father **wearing her mother's
     wedding gown.**   13._____

14. Despite her sincerity and honesty, the candidate failed to **carefully and
     completely** explain why she dropped out of the campaign.   14._____

15. I painted the front door **in my good short set** and ended up ruining the outfit.   15._____

16. Send, **after you have received all of the donations,** the total amount to the
     organization's headquarters.   16._____

17. **Only** one teacher seems able to convince Raymond that he should study.   17._____

18. Only a few Olympic athletes can expect lucrative endorsement contracts **with
     gold medals.**   18._____

19. We watched the *Queen Elizabeth II* as she slowly sailed out to sea **from our
     hotel window.**   19._____

20. Indicate **on the enclosed sheet** whether you are going to the class picnic.   20._____

21. A **battered** man's hat was hanging on a branch of the tree.   21._____

22. Sam, **running out in his robe and slippers to get the morning newspaper on cold January morning,** slammed the front door shut and then realized that he was locked out. 22._____

23. Olympic swimmers often shave off their body hair **that are intent on winning their races.** 23._____

24. Albino Ruales said **when he realized that his grandmother was moving in with his family** that many households are now multi-generational. 24._____

25. He replied that they went to Paris **usually** in the spring. 25._____

39. GRAMMAR: DANGLING MODIFIERS

(Study 29D, Dangling Modifiers)

Write **1** if the boldface words are used **correctly**.
Write **0** if they are used **incorrectly (dangling)**.

Example: Dancing to stardom, fame is an elusive goal.   _____0_____

1. **Announcing his first baseball game in 1939,** the late Red Barber began a broadcasting career that would last over fifty years.   1._____

2. **Rowing across the lake,** the moon often disappeared behind the clouds.   2._____

3. **Having worked on my paper for three hours,** the network went down and my paper was lost in cyberspace.   3._____

4. **While on vacation,** the idea for a new play came to him.   4._____

5. **Worried about what books their children are borrowing from libraries,** the library finally agreed to develop an on-line rating system for families.   5._____

6. **Upon entering college,** he applied for part-time employment in the library.   6._____

7. **Practicing every day for five hours,** Dani's expensive music lessons really paid off.   7._____

8. **Sleeping in late,** the house seemed incredibly quiet with the boys still in bed.   8._____

9. **After sleeping in until noon,** the day seemed to go by too quickly.   9._____

10. **When nine years old,** my father took my sister and me on our first camping trip.   10._____

11. **At the age of ten,** I was permitted to go, for the first time, to a summer camp.   11._____

12. **After putting away my fishing equipment,** the surface of the lake became choppy.   12._____

13. **Racing toward the primate section of the zoo,** the chimpanzees' playful laughter drew the children to their cage.   13._____

14. **To achieve a goal,** a person must expect to work and to make sacrifices.   14._____

15. **Suggesting that the American standard of living has declined,** many American economists predict a gloomy financial status for the next generation.   15._____

16. **After hearing of Tom's need for financial aid,** a hundred dollars was put at his disposal.   16._____

17. **Pickled in spiced vinegar,** the host thought the peaches would go with the meat.   17._____

18. **While running in a local marathon,** the weather was quite uncooperative.   18._____

19. **Relieved by her high grade on the first paper,** the next paper didn't seem as difficult.   19._____

20. **To be a happy puppy,** you need to exercise your pet regularly.   20._____

21. **As a teenager,** Darlene worked two jobs to help her family financially.   21._____

22. **After eating too much chocolate,** my scale revealed that I had gained ten pounds.   22._____

23. Finally, **after working for days,** the garden was free of weeds.   23. _____

24. **To proofread my paper,** I reread it several times and used the grammar and spell-checking functions of my word processing software.   24. _____

25. **After finishing my assignment,** the dog ate it.   25. _____

40. GRAMMAR: DANGLING MODIFIERS

(Study 29D, Dangling Modifiers)

Write **1** if the boldface words are used **correctly**.
Write **0** if the boldface words are used **incorrectly**.

Example: **After dancing the lead in *Swan Lake*,** cheers filled the hall.   0

1.   **Writing during the Renaissance,** poems were characterized as speaking pictures.   1._____

2.   **Approaching New York,** the view of the Manhattan skyline was exciting.   2._____

3.   **To get ready for summer vacation,** camp registrations had to be completed this week.   3._____

4.   **After searching the attic for several days,** the missing antique lamp was found.   4._____

5.   **Realizing the unemployment rate is still over 10 percent,** most workers are not changing jobs.   5._____

6.   **Worried about getting into medical school,** Nina decided to study more.   6._____

7.   **Hearing the weather report,** I decided to leave for work an hour earlier than usual.   7._____

8.   **To get a passing grade in this course,** the professor's little quirks must be considered.   8._____

9.   **While working on the computer,** David's youngest son played with his blocks.   9._____

10. **Having read the morning paper,** I tossed it aside and started the laundry.   10._____

41. GRAMMAR: REVIEW

(Study 1-29, Grammar)

Write **1** for each statement that is **true**.
Write **0** for each that is **false**.

Example: A **present participle** is a word that ends in *-ing* and is used as an adjective. _____1_____

1. Both a **gerund** and a **present participle** end in *-ing*. 1. _____

2. The greatest number of words ever used in a **verb** is four. 2. _____

3. **Parallel structure** is used to designate ideas that are not equal in importance. 3. _____

4. A **dangling participle** may be corrected by being changed into a dependent clause. 4. _____

5. *It's* is a contraction of *it is; its* is the **possessive** form of the pronoun *its*. 5. _____

6. The **predicate precedes the subject** in a sentence beginning with the expletive *there*. 6. _____

7. A **preposition** may contain two or more words; *because of* is an example. 7. _____

8. The **principal parts of a verb** are the *present tense*, the *future tense,* and the *past participle*. 8. _____

9. A **collective noun** may be followed by either a singular or plural verb. 9. _____

10. A **prepositional phrase** may be used only as an adjective modifier. 10. _____

11. A **compound sentence** is one that contains two or more independent clauses. 11. _____

12. Not all **adverbs** end in *-ly*. 12. _____

13. *To lie* is an **intransitive verb**; *to lay* is a **transitive verb** and is always followed by a direct object. 13. _____

14. A **noun clause** may be introduced by the subordinate conjunction *although*. 14. _____

15. An **adjective clause** may begin with *when* or *where*. 15. _____

16. Both **verbals** and **verbs** may have modifiers and complements. 16. _____

17. The terminal punctuation of a declarative sentence is the **exclamation point**. 17. _____

18. *Without* is a **subordinate conjunction**. 18. _____

19. A sentence may begin with the word *because*. 19. _____

20. The **predicate** of a sentence can consist of merely a past participle. 20. _____

21. A **subjective complement** may be a noun, a pronoun, or an adverb. 21. _____

22. A **direct object** may be a noun or a pronoun. 22. _____

23. An **indirect object** always follows a direct object. 23. _____

24. An **objective complement** always precedes the direct object. 24. _____

25. Pronouns used as appositives are called **intensive pronouns.** 25. _____

26. The word *scissors* takes a **singular verb.** 26. _____

27. An **antecedent** is the noun for which a pronoun stands.   27. _____

28. A **simple sentence** contains two or more independent clauses.   28. _____

29. Pronouns in the **objective case** always follow forms of the verb *to be*.   29. _____

30. A **complex sentence** contains at least one independent clause and one dependent clause.   30. _____

31. A **sentence fragment** is not considered a legitimate unit of expression; a **nonsentence** is.   31. _____

32. **Adjectives** never stand next to the words they modify.   32. _____

33. Not all words ending in *-ly* are **adverbs**.   33. _____

34. An **indefinite pronoun** designates no particular person.   34. _____

35. The words *have* and *has* identify the **present perfect tense** of a verb.   35. _____

36. A statement with a subject and a verb can be a fragment if it follows a **subordinate conjunction.**   36. _____

37. An **adverb** may modify a noun, an adjective, or another adverb.   37. _____

38. **Verbs** are words that assert an action or a state of being.   38. _____

39. The **indicative mood** of a verb is used to express a command or a request.   39. _____

40. The function of a **subordinate conjunction** is to join a dependent clause to a main clause.   40. _____

41. The **subjective mood** expresses doubt, uncertainty, a wish, or a supposition.   41. _____

42. An **adjective** may modify a noun, a pronoun, or an adverb.   42. _____

43. A **gerund** is a word ending in *-ing* and used as a noun.   43. _____

44. A **clause** differs from a **phrase** in that a clause always has a subject and a predicate.   44. _____

45. **Adjectives** tell *what kind, how many,* or *which one;* **adverbs** tell *when, where, how,* and *to what degree.*   45. _____

46. A **comma splice** is a grammatical error caused by joining two independent clauses with a comma.   46. _____

47. **Coordinate conjunctions** *(and, but, or, nor, for, yet)* join words, phrases, and clauses of equal importance.   47. _____

48. **Pronouns in the objective case** *(him, me, etc.)* should be used as direct objects of verbs and verbals.   48. _____

49. A **fused sentence** is an error caused by joining two independent clauses with a comma.   49. _____

50. A **simple short sentence** can be a forceful expression in a passage.   50. _____

Write **1** if the sentence is **correct**. Write **0** if it is **incorrect**.

Example: Was that letter sent to Paul or I?   ___0___

1. **Having been notified to come at once,** there was no opportunity to call you.   1. _____

2. I suspected that his remarks were directed to Larry and **me.**   2. _____

3. He, **thinking that he might find his friends on the second floor of the library,** hurried. 3. _____

4. If a student attends the review session, **they** will do well on the first exam. 4. _____

5. In the cabin of the boat **was** a radio, a set of flares, and a map of the area. 5. _____

6. The Queen, standing beside her husband, children, and grandchildren, **were** waving regally at the crowd. 6. _____

7. She is a person **who** I think is certain to succeed as a social worker. 7. _____

8. **Is** there any other questions you wish to ask regarding the assignment? 8. _____

9. **Do** either of you use the Internet? 9. _____

10. He particularly enjoys **playing softball** and **to run** a mile every morning. 10. _____

11. Forward the complaint to **whoever** you think is in charge. 11. _____

12. Every girl and boy **was** to have an opportunity to try out for the soccer team. 12. _____

13. Neither the bus driver nor the passengers **were** aware of their danger. 13. _____

14. Within the next five years, personal computers will be **not only** smaller **but also** more affordable. 14. _____

15. Not everyone feels that **their** life is better since the 1960s civil rights movement. 15. _____

16. Homemade bread tastes **differently** from bakery bread. 16. _____

17. Not **having had** the chance to consult his lawyer, Larry refused to answer the officer's questions. 17. _____

18. **Is** either of your friends interested in going to Florida over spring break? 18. _____

19. He enrolled in economics **because** it had always been of interest to him. 19. _____

20. Jacob read **steady** for two weeks before he finished his novel. 20. _____

21. Burt paced nervously up and down the corridor. **Because he was concerned about the weather.** 21. _____

22. **A heavy rain began without warning,** the crew struggled with the tarpaulin. 22. _____

23. **To have better control over spending,** the checkbook is balanced each week. 23. _____

24. Casey **asked for time, stepped out of the batter's box, and his finger was pointed** toward the bleachers. 24. _____

25. The interview committee could not make up **its** mind regarding which applicant to hire. 25. _____

42. PUNCTUATION: THE COMMA

(Study 30-32, The Comma)

If **no comma** is needed in the bracketed space(s), write **0**. If **one or more** commas are needed, write in the number (**1** to **10** from the list below) of the **reason** for the comma(s). (Use only one number for each answer.)

1. independent clauses joined by and, but, or, nor, for, yet
2. introductory adverb clause
3. series
4. parenthetical expression(other than nonrestrictive clause)
5. nonrestrictive clause

6. appositve
7. absolute phrase
8 direct address
9. mild interjection
10. direct quotation

Example: Donald's nephews are Huey( )Duey( ) and Louie.   ___3___

1. *The Mysterious Assaults From Hell*( ) a book by Deodat Lawson( ) narrates what the author observed at 1692 Salem witch trials.   1._____

2. Professors( ) who assign too many long papers( ) may have small classes.   2._____

3. Well( ) I guess we'll have to leave without Ida.   3._____

4. If there are no other questions( ) let's begin our game.   4._____

5. So you see( ) Dr. Haywood( ) I can't possibly pay your bill by next week.   5._____

6. Phillip's father( ) who is a religious man( ) disapproves of many teenage antics. 6._____

7. Dan and Marilyn( ) however( ) are hopeful for a 1996 victory.   7._____

8. John Fitgerald Kennedy( ) the thirty-fifth President of the United States( ) was assassinated on November 22, 1963.   8._____

9. The Chinese are trained to write with their right hands( ) for it is difficult to do Chinese calligraphy with the left hand.   9._____

10. Before you meet clients for the first time( ) learn all that you can about their company, their style, and their risk-taking ability.   10._____

11. He sat down at his desk last evening( ) and made a preliminary draft of his speech. 11._____

12. Julie went into the library( ) but she hurried out a few minutes later.   12._____

13. Lincoln spoke eloquently about government of the people( ) by the people( ) and for the people.   13._____

14. After she had listened to her favorite album( ) she settled down to study.   14._____

15. The candidate gave a number of speeches in Illinois( ) where she hoped to win support.   15._____

16. She has always wanted to visit the small village( ) where her father had lived. 16._____

17. My instructor( ) Dr. Ursula Tyler( ) outlined the work for the current semester. 17._____

18. What you need( ) David( ) is a professional organizer to straighten out your office. 18._____

19. "Is this( )" she asked( ) "the only excuse that you have to offer?"   19._____

20. Castles were cold and filthy( ) according to historians( ) because castles were built more for protection than convenience.

20. ＿＿＿＿＿

21. His hands swollen from five fire ant bites( ) John swore that he would rid his yard of all ant hills.

21. ＿＿＿＿＿

22. Yes( ) both potato and corn crops had a major impact on the life expectancy of Europeans living in the eighteenth century.

22. ＿＿＿＿＿

23. Ford's first Model T sold for $850 in 1908( ) but the price dropped to $440 in 1915 because of mass production.

23. ＿＿＿＿＿

24. We were asked to read *The Grapes of Wrath*( ) which is a novel by John Steinbeck.

24. ＿＿＿＿＿

25. Lorraine Hansberry( ) the author of *A Raisin in the Sun*( ) died at thirty-five.

25. ＿＿＿＿＿

43. PUNCTUATION: THE COMMA

(Study 30-32, The Comma)

If **no comma** is needed in the bracketed space(s), write **0**. If **one or more** commas are needed, write in the number (**1** to **10** from the list below) of the **reason** for the comma(s). (Use only one number for each answer.)

1. parenthetical expression
2. nonrestrictive clause
3. direct address
4. after *yes* and *no*
5. before *such as, especially,* or *particularly*

6. contrast
7. omission
8. confirmatory question
9. date
10. state or country

Example: The Allies invaded Normandy on June 6 ( ) 1944.   ____9____

1. Our house( ) which was built in 1928( ) needs new electrical wiring.   1._____

2. Senator( ) would you comment on reports that you will not run again?   2._____

3. Menlo Park( ) New Jersey( ) was Edison's home.   3._____

4. Seashells are an exquisite natural sculpture( ) aren't they?   4._____

5. The decision to have the surgery( ) of course( ) should be based on several doctors' opinions.   5._____

6. I hope( ) Charles and Mary( ) that you will come to see us often.   6._____

7. The person( ) who wrote that note to you( ) needs a lesson in manners!   7._____

8. For this production, John played Robert; Judith( ) Harriet.   8._____

9. Is it true( ) sir( ) that you are unwilling to be interviewed by the press? 9._____

10. Marisa Martinez came all the way from San Antonio( ) Texas( ) to attend college in Cleveland.   10._____

11. Frank graduated from the University of Michigan; Esther( ) from Columbia University. 11._____

12. Students( ) who work their way through college( ) learn to value their college training. 12._____

13. She said, "No( ) I absolutely refuse to answer your question."   13._____

14. The Latin American geography has many types of terrain( ) such as lowlands, rain forests, vast plains, high plateaus, and fertile valleys.   14._____

15. On October 11( ) 1985( ) our adopted son arrived from Korea.   15._____

16. The film had been advertised as a children's movie( ) not a production full of violence. 16._____

17. We were fortunate( ) nevertheless( ) to have recovered all of our luggage.   17._____

18. The average person in the Middle Ages never owned a book( ) or even saw one. 18._____

19. You will join us at the art museum( ) won't you?   19._____

20. I've already told you( ) little boy( ) that I'm not giving back your ball.   20._____

21. Ralph Ellison( ) who wrote *The Invisible Man*( ) is also well known for his essays, interviews, and speeches.   21._____

22. Not everyone( ) who objected to the new ruling( ) signed the petition.   22._____

23. It was( ) on the other hand( ) an opportunity that he could not turn down.   23._____

24. Dwight Eisenhower( ) who was our thirty-fourth President( ) was born on October 14, 1890.   24._____

25. She has several hobbies( ) such as collecting coins, writing verse, and growing roses.   25._____

44. PUNCTUATION: THE COMMA

(Study 30-32, The Comma)

If no comma is needed in the bracketed space(s), write **0**. **If one or more commas** are needed, write in the number (**1** through **11** from the list below) of the **reason** for the comma(s). (Use only one number for each answer.)

1. independent clauses joined by and, but, for, or, nor, so, yet
2. introductory adverb clause
3. long introductory prepositional phrase
4. introductory participial phrase
5. introductory infinitive phrase
6. series

7. coordinate adjectives
8. appositive
9. absolute phrase
10. mild interjection
11. direct quotation

Example: James Joyce( ) Ireland's most famous novelist( ) lived most of his life abroad.   ___8___

1. The Browns have good running backs( ) and look good on defense as well.   1._____

2. Well( ) we'll probably see another foot of snow before the winter ends.   2._____

3. Agatha Christie( ) the famous mystery writer( ) caricatured herself in her books.   3._____

4. Convinced of her client's innocence( ) the young lawyer searched for additional reliable witnesses.   4._____

5. The concert having ended( ) the fans rushed toward the stage.   5._____

6. He hoped to write short stories( ) publish his poems( ) and plan a novel.   6._____

7. If the fog continues( ) we'll have to postpone our trip.   7._____

8. Many people had tried to reach the top of the mountain( ) yet only a few had succeeded.   8._____

9. Equipped with only an inexpensive camera( ) she succeeded in taking a prize-winning picture.   9._____

10. During times of emotional distress and heightened tensions( ) Lee remains calm.   10._____

11. To prepare for her finals( ) Cathy studied in the library all week.   11._____

12. Recognizing that his position was hopeless( ) James resigned.   12._____

13. Airbags in cars have saved many lives during crashes( ) but they can be dangerous for children under twelve.   13._____

14. Mr. Novak found himself surrounded by noisy( ) exuberant students.   14._____

15. "We are( )" she said( ) "prepared to serve meals to a group of considerable size."   15._____

16. Judy had no intention of withdrawing from college( ) nor was she willing to carry a lighter program.   16._____

17. To improve a child's diet( ) add more beans and green vegetables to the meal.   17._____

18. Although Derek was an excellent driver( ) he still had difficulty finding a sponsor for the race.   18._____

19.   "You must be more quiet( ) or the landlord will make us move," she said.   19. _____

20.   Dave Smithers( ) the sophomore class president( ) campaigned for an increase in campus activities.   20. _____

21.   I could not decide whether to attend college( ) or to travel to Nigeria with my aunt.   21. _____

22.   Built on a high cliff( ) the house afforded a panoramic view of the valley below.   22. _____

23.   Our phone constantly ringing( ) we decided to rely on the answering machine to avoid interruptions during supper.   23. _____

24.   The professor raised his voice to a low roar( ) the class having apparently dozed off.   24. _____

25.   Her courses included Russian( ) organic chemistry( ) and marine biology.   25. _____

45. PUNCTUATION: THE COMMA

(Study 30-32, The Comma)

Write **1** if the punctuation in parenthese is **correct**;
Write **0** if it is **incorrect**.

(Use only one number for each answer.)

Example: We would appreciate it(,) therefore(,) if you paid our bill and left.   ___1___

1.   She died(,) because she had been unable to find shelter.   1. _____

2.   We traveled to Idaho(,) and went down the Snake River.   2. _____

3.   "Tell me," he demanded(,) "who you are."   3. _____

4.   When the results were in(,) Marvin was the winner.   4. _____

5.   You expect to graduate in June(,) don't you?   5. _____

6.   O'Conner started the second half at linebacker(,) Bryant having torn his
     knee ligaments.   6. _____

7.   O'Conner started the second half at linebacker(,) Bryant had torn his knee ligaments.   7. _____

8.   Trying to concentrate(,) Susan closed the door and turned off the television set.   8. _____

9.   "Americans(,) I look forward to the opportunity to serve this country," he said.   9. _____

10. Some of the older and more conservative members of the organization(,) were
     shocked by Roseanna's speech.   10. _____

11. Helen, who especially enjoys baseball, sat in the front row(,) and watched the
     game closely.   11. _____

12. "Are you going to a fire?"(,) the police officer asked the speeding motorist.   12. _____

13. Two of the students left the office(,) the third waited to see the dean.   13. _____

14. Angela and two of her friends(,) recently performed at the student talent show.   14. _____

15. "I won't wait any longer," she said(,) picking up her books from the bench.   15. _____

16. The tough(,) angry attitude was only a way to prevent others from knowing how
     scared he was about failing.   16. _____

17. The relatively short drought(,) nonetheless(,) had still caused much damage to
     the crops.   17. _____

18. The apartment they rented(,) had no screens or storm windows.   18. _____

19. According to the polls, the candidate was losing(,) he blamed the media for
     the results.   19. _____

20. However(,) much you may think you like ice cream, two quarts will be too much.   20. _____

21. In Williamsport, Pennsylvania(,) in June 1972, many people lost their homes
     because of severe flooding.   21. _____

22. "Did you know," the financial aid officer replied(,) "that each year thousands of scholarships go unclaimed?"

22. _____

23. Her English professor(,) who was having difficulty getting to class on time(,) requested that the class move to a different building.

23. _____

24. F. Scott Fitzgerald(,) the author of *The Great Gatsby*(,) grew up in Minnesota.

24. _____

25. Next summer she hopes to fulfill a lifelong wish(,) to travel to Alaska by ship.

25. _____

26. First-graders now engage in writing journals(,) in problem-solving activities(,) and in brief science experiments.

26. _____

27. Her last day in the office(,) was spent in sorting papers and filing manuscripts.

27. _____

28. In preparation for the party(,) Carla began cleaning and cooking a week earlier.

28. _____

29. Having loaded her word processor(,) Colleen began her great American novel.

29. _____

30. Haven't you any idea(,) of the responsibility involved in running a household?

30. _____

31. Even though the young soldier believed in democracy, he didn't want to go to war.

31. _____

32. Shaking hands with his patient, the physician asked(,) "Now what kind of surgery are we doing today?"

32. _____

33. No( ) I don't want another cat.

33. _____

34. Erron and Nakita determined to find a less painful(,) but effective diet.

34. _____

35. The American cowboys' hat actually had many purposes besides shielding their faces from the sun and rain(,) for many cowboys used their hat as a pillow and a drinking cup.

35. _____

36. During conversations about controversial topics(,) our faces often communicate our thoughts, especially our emotional responses.

36. _____

37. Harry Rosen(,) a skilled, polished speaker(,) effectively used humor during his speeches.

37. _____

38. To understand how living arrangements affect student relationships(,) the psychology department completed several informal observational studies on campus.

38. _____

39. Peter's goal was to make a short movie in graduate school(,) and not to worry about future career goals.

39. _____

40. The states with the largest numbers of dairy cows are Wisconsin(,) California(,) and New York.

40. _____

41. Young Soo's mother was preparing *kimchi*(,) a pickled cabbage dish that is commonly eaten with Korean meals.

41. _____

42. Having friends must be an important aspect of our culture(,) for many popular television series focus on how a group of characters care for their friendships with one another.

42. _____

43. People beginning an intimate relationship use a significant number of affectionate expressions(,) but the frequency of these expressions drop as the relationship matures.

43. _____

44. Working hard to pay the mortgage, to educate their children, and to save money for retirement(,) many of America's middle class now call themselves the "new poor."

44. _____

45. The children could take martial arts classes near home(,) or they could decide to save their money for summer camp.

45. _____

46. Now only 68 percent of American children live with both biological parents(,) 20 percent of children live in single-parent families(,) and 9 percent live with one biological parent and a step-parent.

46. _____

47. Jeff was hungry for a gooey(,) chocolate brownie smothered in whipped cream and chocolate sauce.

47. _____

48. His thoughts overwhelmed with grief(,) Jack decided to postpone his vacation for another month.

48. _____

49. "Oh(,) I forgot to bring my report home to finish it tonight," sighed Mary.

49. _____

50. People exercise because it makes them feel good(,) they may even become addicted to exercise.

50. _____

46. PUNCTUATION: THE COMMA

(Study 30-32, The Comma)

Parentheses have been inserted in each sentence to indicate where a comma **could be placed**. Determine how many commas should be inserted. Write the number of commas needed. If there should be **no commas** in the sentence, select **0** as the answer.

Example: "I'll have a hamburger( ) fries( ) and a coke( ) with lots of ice."   ___2___

1. College students need( ) a good dictionary( ) a desk( ) and some patience and enthusiasm to succeed in their first composition class.   1._____

2. Because of the dramatic increase( ) in medical costs in America( ) many Americans have not been able( ) to afford immunization( ) for their children.   2._____

3. According to Robert Darnton's research( ) the story of "Little Red Riding Hood( )" may reveal( ) some information( ) about the anxieties and issues of eighteenth-century French peasants.   3._____

4. Women( ) will you( ) allow more movies( ) depicting violence against your sisters( ) to be produced?   4._____

5. I wanted( ) to go( ) to Harvard; Terry( ) to Yale.   5._____

6. I( ) didn't realize( ) that four Latin American writers( ) have won the Nobel Prize for Literature.   6._____

7. Unlike the Maya( ) and Aztecs( ) the Incas had no written language( ) but instead they kept records on knotted strings( ) called *quipus*.   7._____

8. The chairman( ) who had already served two terms in Congress( ) and one in the State Assembly( ) declared his candidacy again.   8._____

9. Jack was born on December 1( ) 1965( ) in Fargo( ) North Dakota( ) during a blizzard.   9._____

10. I consider him( ) to be( ) a hard-working student but( ) I may be wrong.   10._____

11. Audrey( ) a woman( ) whom I met last summer( ) is here( ) to see me.   11._____

12. Having an interest( ) in anthropology( ) she frequently audited( ) Dr. Irwin's class( ) that met on Saturdays.   12._____

13. Native Americans were the first to grow corn( ) potatoes( ) squash( ) pumpkins( ) and avocados.   13._____

14. Well( ) I dislike her intensely( ) but( ) she is quite clever( ) to be sure.   14._____

15. To solve( ) her legal problems( ) she consulted an attorney( ) that she knew( ) from college.   15._____

16. "To what( )" he asked( ) "do you attribute( ) your great popularity( ) with the students?"   16._____

17. From Native Americans( ) the world learned about cinnamon( ) and chocolate( ) and about chicle( ) the main ingredient in chewing gum.   17._____

18. "Blowing in the Wind( )" a folk song written by Bob Dylan( ) in 1962( ) promises( ) that life will get better through time.   18._____

19. Many filmmakers are creating( ) serious movies( ) about their cultural heritage; however, there are( ) few commercially successful movies about Asian American cultures.

19. _____

20. "You haven't seen my glasses( ) have you?" Granny asked( ) the twins( ) thinking they had hidden them( ) somewhere in the living room.

20. _____

21. The car having broken down( ) because of a dirty carburetor( ) we missed the first act( ) in which( ) Hamlet confronts his father's ghost.

21. _____

22. After she had paid her tuition( ) she checked in at the residence hall( ) that she had selected( ) and soon began( ) unloading her suitcases and boxes.

22. _____

23. The day was so warm( ) and sunny( ) that the entire class wished fervently( ) that the lecture would take place( ) outdoors.

23. _____

24. Chinese porcelain( ) which is prized for its beauty( ) and its translucence( ) was copied( ) by seventeenth-century Dutch potters.

24. _____

25. The road to Brattleboro( ) being coated with ice( ) we proceeded( ) slowly( ) and cautiously.

25. _____

47. PUNCTUATION: THE COMMA

(Study 30-32, The Comma)

The following sentences **either** need a comma **or** contain an incorrectly used comma.
First, write the word **after** which a comma needs to be placed **or** after which a comma needs to be removed.
Next, write the number of the reason for making your correction from the list below: The sentence needs a comma because there is(are):

1. two independent clauses joined by and, but, for, or, nor, so, yet
2. an introductory adverb clause
3. an introductory phrase (long prepositional, participial, infinitive, or absolute)
4. a series
5. an appositive
6. a nonrestrictive clause or phrase.

The comma that is there now is wrong because:

7. there is no full clause after the conjunction.
8. the comma separates the subject from its verb.
9. the comma separates the verb from its complement.
10. there is a restrictive (or essential) clause.

Example: When Frank and Joe looked around the stranger had vanished.   __around__ __2__

Example: The sun, shone brightly.   __sun__ __8__

1. There was much to do before her guests arrived for dinner but Betty did not know where to begin.   1. _____ ____

2. That it is indeed, time for extremely serious commitment and concerted action on your part seems evident.   2. _____ ____

3. Having examined and reexamined the ancient manuscript the committee of scholars declared it genuine.   3. _____ ____

4. If the weather is pleasant and dry, we will march in the St. Patrick's Day parade, and then dance at a parish party.   4. _____ ____

5. Amanda has decided to write a cookbook, remodel her kitchen and travel through California.   5. _____ ____

6. Many Americans now prefer news stories, that offer human interest stories.   6. _____ ____

7. The country, that receives the most media attention often is the recipient of the most aid from the United Nations.   7. _____ ____

8. Coaching soccer, and teaching part-time at a local college keep me quite busy.   8. _____ ____

9. George and Robert thoroughly and painstakingly considered, what had to be done to defuse the bomb.   9. _____ ____

10. If ever there was the law on one side, and simple justice on the other, here is such a situation.   10. _____ ____

11. Ann Tyler, who won a Pulitzer Prize in 1988 has recently written a novel about a woman in her forties who runs away from her family.

11. _____ ____

12. Barbara Bush, will be remembered as a First Lady who cared for her family and for her country.

12. _____ ____

13. Claiming that he was just offering good advice Ace frequently would tell me which card to play.

13. _____ ____

14. What gave Helen the inspiration for her short story, was her mother's account of growing up on a farm.

14. _____ ____

15. Owen's baseball cards included such famous examples as Willie Mays's running catch in the 1954 World Series, and Hank Aaron's record-breaking home run.

15. _____ ____

16. The volume that was the most valuable in the library's rare book collection, was a First Folio edition of Shakespeare's plays.

16. _____ ____

17. *Gone With The Wind* a film enjoyed by millions of people throughout the world, was first thought unlikely to be a commercial success.

17. _____ ____

18. Because the material was difficult to understand Monica decided to hire a tutor.

18. _____ ____

19. Baseball player Don Baylor had 255 hits, and batted in 1,276 runs during his major league career.

19. _____ ____

20. Although everyone was ready for the test no one complained when Professor Smith canceled the test.

20. _____ ____

48. PUNCTUATION: THE PERIOD, QUESTION MARK, AND EXCLAMATION POINT

(Study 33-34, the Period; 35-36, The Question; and 37-38, The Exclamation Mark)

Write **1** if the punctuation inside the brackets is **correct**.
Write **0** if it is **incorrect**.

Example: Are we having fun yet[?]		1
1.	You'd like that, wouldn't you[?]	1._____
2.	"Evacuate the dorm; there's a fire!" the resident assisted shouted[!]	2._____
3.	The police officer calmly inquired if I had the slightest notion of just how fast I was backing up[?]	3._____
4.	Mr. Hall and Miss[.] James will chair the committee.	4._____
5.	The chem[.] test promises to be challenging.	5._____
6.	Where is the office? Down the hall on the left[.]	6._____
7.	Good afternoon, ma'am[.] May I present you will a free scrub brush?	7._____
8.	"How much did the owners spend on players' salaries?" the reporter asked[?]	8._____
9.	His next question—wouldn't you know[?]—was, "What do you need, ma'am?"	9._____
10.	"Wow! Your computer even has a video camera[!]"	10._____
11.	"What a magnificent view you have of the mountains[!]" said he.	11._____
12.	Who said, "If at first you don't succeed, try, try again" [?]	12._____
13.	Would you please check my computer for viruses[?]	13._____
14.	HELP WANTED: Editor[.] for our new brochure.	14._____
15.	Pat, please type this memo[.] to the purchasing department.	15._____
16.	What? You lent that scoundrel Snively $10,000[?!]	16._____
17.	I asked her why, of all the men on campus, she had chosen him[?]	17._____
18.	Why did I do it? Because I respected her[.] Jackie worked hard to finish her degree.	18._____
19.	Footloose and Fancy Free[.] [title of an essay]	19._____
20.	Would you please send me your reply by e-mail[.]	20._____
21.	Your cat ate my goldfish[!!] Why didn't you tell me he was a murdering feline?	21._____
22.	Charlie was an inspiring [?] date. He burped all through dinner.	22._____
23.	My supervisor asked how much equipment I would need to update the computer center[.]	23._____
24.	The essay was "Computers: Can We Live Without Them[?]"	24._____
25.	I heard the news on station W[.]I[.]N[.]K.	25._____

49. PUNCTUATION: THE SEMICOLON

(Study 39, The Semicolon)

Using the following list, write the number of the **reason** for the semicolon in each sentence. (Use only one number for each sentence.)

1. between independent clauses not joined by any conjunction or conjunctive adverb
2. between independent clauses joined by a conjunctive adverb (however, therefore, etc.)
3. between clauses joined by and, but, for, or, nor, so, or yet but having internal commas
4. to group items in a series

Example: Everyone predicts the Indians will win the World Series; John still insists that the
other team will be victorious.   _____1_____

1. Congress has now voted to spend more to protect wildlife; however, it may be already
    too late for many species.   1._____

2. The farmers are using an improved fertilizer; thus their crop yields have increased.   2._____

3. Still to come were Perry, a trained squirrel; Arnold, an acrobat; and Mavis, a magician.   3._____

4. "Negotiations," he said, "have collapsed; we will strike at noon."   4._____

5. Study the manual carefully before the quiz; the lab instructor draws the questions
    from the manual.   5._____

6. The average Internet user spends about six hours a week online; the majority of
    these users reach the Internet from work.   6._____

7. Pam, who lives in the suburbs, drives her car to work each day; yet Ruben,
    her next-door neighbor, takes the bus.   7._____

8. Changing your time management habits requires determination; therefore, begin by
    writing down your goals.   8._____

9. The play was produced in Altoona, Pennsylvania; Buckhannon, West Virginia;
    and The Woodlands, Texas.   9._____

10. The Chicago-based alternative band, the Smashing Pumpkins, is quite popular;
    the band's songs use a variety of musical expressions.   10._____

If **a semicolon** is needed within the brackets, insert it; then in the blank at
the right, write the number (**1** to **4** from the list above) of the reason for than semicolon.
If **no semicolon** is needed within the brackets, write **0** in the blank. (Use only one number in each blank.)

Example: I couldn't help you with your assignment[ ] moreover, I wouldn't.   _____2_____

1. The Puritans banned the Christmas holiday when they settled in North
    America [ ] the holiday wasn't revived until the 1880s.   1._____

2. Shall I telephone to find out the time [ ] when the box office opens?   2._____

3. A recent study indicates that saccharin does not cause cancer in humans [ ] the only consumers who should worry are laboratory rats.

3. _____

4. Louise read the help wanted ads [ ] and went to the campus employment office for weeks until, to her great relief, she found a summer job.

4. _____

5. She is very bright [ ] at twenty, she is the owner of a successful small business.

5. _____

6. The surprises in the team's starting lineup were Garcia, the second baseman [ ] Hudler, the shortstop [ ] and Fitzgerald, the catcher.

6. _____

7. The national public education system needs to redefine its expectations [ ] because most schools do not expect all of their students to succeed.

7. _____

8. Hollywood has always portrayed the Union soldiers as dressed in blue and the Confederate troops in gray [ ] however, for the first year of the Civil War, most soldiers wore their state militia uniforms, which came in many colors.

8. _____

9. Soft drinks are a traditional beverage in the United States [ ] flavored soda water first appeared in 1825 in Philadelphia.

9. _____

10. Orville and Wilbur Wright were an odd pair to revolutionize travel [ ] for they ran a bicycle shop in Dayton, had no scientific training, and never finished high school.

10. _____

50. PUNCTUATION: THE SEMICOLON AND THE COMMA

(Study 30-32, The Comma; and 39, The Semicolon)

Decide whether a comma, a semicolon, or nothing is needed within the brackets.

Write **1** if you would insert a **comma** within the brackets.
Write **2** if you would insert a **semicolon**.
Write **0** if you would insert **nothing**.

Example: The referee dropped the puck[ ] then the game began while the fans stood up and cheered.   ____2____

1. Scientists are using sophisticated radio telescopes to survey distant celestial bodies[ ] they hope to hear signals from intelligent life.   1._____

2. Most Americans plan financially for retirement[ ] but many retire earlier than expected.   2._____

3. Dr. Jones[ ] who teaches geology[ ] graduated from MIT.   3._____

4. The Dr. Jones [ ] who teaches geology[ ] graduated from MIT.   4._____

5. I met the woman[ ] who is to be president of the new junior college.   5._____

6. She likes working in Washington, D.C.[ ] she hopes to remain there permanently.   6._____

7. For the teenagers, the program was entertaining[ ] for the adults, it was boring.   7._____

8. Read the article carefully[ ] then write an essay on the author's handling of the subject.   8._____

9. The car company has produced a car paint[ ] that turns different colors depending on the light.   9._____

10. The game being beyond our reach[ ] the coach told me to start warming up.   10._____

11. We're going on a cruise around the bay on Sunday[ ] and we'd like you to come with us.   11._____

12. If Amy decides to become a lawyer[ ] you can be sure she'll be a good one.   12._____

13. Customer satisfaction is important[ ] therefore, the owners hired a consulting firm to conduct a customer survey.   13._____

14. Li-Young registered for an advanced biology course[ ] otherwise, she might not have been admitted to medical school.   14._____

15. Many companies [ ] however[ ] are now using handwriting analysts to screen job applicants.   15._____

16. Portable phones are popular with most families[ ] but many of these phones don't work well in crowded urban areas.   16._____

17. He began his speech again[ ] fire engines having drowned out his opening remarks. 17._____

18. The best day of the vacation occurred[ ] when we took the kids sled riding.   18._____

19. Let me introduce the new officers: Phillip Whitaker, president [ ] Elaine Donatelli, secretary[ ] and Pierre Northrup, treasurer.   19._____

20. We thought of every possible detail when planning the dinner party[ ] yet we didn't anticipate our cat's jumping into the cake.   20. _____

21. We had know the Floyd Archers[ ] ever since they moved here from New Jersey.   21. _____

22. During the summer we visited friends in Chicago[ ] New York[ ] and Toronto.   22. _____

23. The drama coach was a serene person[ ] not one to be worried about nervous amateurs.   23. _____

24. To turn them into professional performers was[ ] needless to say[ ] an impossible task.   24. _____

25. "Yes, I will attend the review session," Jack said[ ] "if you can guarantee that the time spent will be worthwhile."   25. _____

26. Call the security office[ ] if there seems to be any problem with the locks.   26. _____

27. Couples with severe disabilities may have difficulty raising a family[ ] because there are few programs to help disabled parents with their children.   27. _____

28. Britain was the first Common Market country to react[ ] others quickly followed suit.   28. _____

29. The tanker ran aground in perfectly fair weather and calm seas[ ] the captain was fired.   29. _____

30. Perhaps because the weather was finally warm again[ ] I didn't want to stay inside.   30. _____

31. American couples are examining their life style[ ] many are cutting back in their work schedules to spend more time with their children.   31. _____

32. The World Series hadn't yet begun[ ] however, he had equipped himself with a new radio.   32. _____

33. I couldn't remember having seen her as radiantly happy[ ] as she now was.   33. _____

34. No, I cannot go to the game[ ] I have a term paper to finish.   34. _____

35. Kristi Yamaguchi [ ] in fact, is a fourth-generation Japanese-American.   35. _____

36. Victor, on the other hand[ ] played the best game of his career.   36. _____

37. Home-grown products aren't that special in rural farming communities[ ] on the other hand, such products can command high prices in urban areas.   37. _____

38. "There will be no rain today[ ]" she insisted. "The weather forecaster says so."   38. _____

39. Swimming is an excellent form of exercise[ ] swimming for 26 minutes consumes 100 calories.   39. _____

40. Although he majored in math in college[ ] he has trouble balancing his checkbook.   40. _____

41. The short story[ ] that impressed me the most[ ] was written by a thirty-five-year-old police officer.   41. _____

42. Mary constantly counts calories and fat content in the food she eats[ ] yet she never loses more than a pound.   42. _____

43. Many cultures follow different calendars[ ] the Jewish New Year is celebrated in the fall, the Vietnamese and Chinese New Year at the beginning of the year, and the Cambodian New Year in April.   43. _____

44. "My fraternity[ ]" stated Travis, "completes numerous community service projects throughout the school year."   44. _____

45. All the students were present for the final[ ] although most were suffering with the flu.   45. _____

46. Muslim students on campus asked the administration for a larger international student center[ ] and a quiet place for their daily prayers.   46. _____

47. Whenever Sam is sad and feeling discouraged about his job[ ] he puts on a Tony Bennett record and dances with the dog.

47._____

48. Barry and I were planning a large farewell party for Eugene within the next month[ ] but certainly not next week.

48._____

49. To read only mysteries and novels[ ] was my plan for the holiday break.

49._____

50. My Amish grandmother always kept a clean, neat house; likewise[ ] my mother also cleaned every day.

50._____

51. PUNCTUATION: THE SEMICOLON AND THE COMMA

(Study 30-32, The Comma; and 39; The Semicolon.)

Decide whether a comma, a semicolon, or nothing is needed within the brackets.

Select **1** if you should insert a **comma** within the brackets.
Select **2** if you should insert a **semicolon**.
Select **0** if you should insert **nothing**.

Example: The television blared [ ] the children sat motionless.   <u> 2 </u>

1. Felicia's father launched into his usual diatribe about the younger generation[ ] the room quickly emptied.   1._____

2. Successful comediennes include Phyllis Diller[ ] Elayne Boosler[ ] and Pam Stone.   2._____

3. "Do you have any idea what will be on the final exam?"[ ] asked the student.   3._____

4. John uses a video conferencing network to conduct business[ ] instead of spending time flying all over the world for meetings.   4._____

5. Many companies are downsizing[ ] employees are either fired or asked to work at home.   5._____

6. Blenchford studied all night[ ] but failed the test.   6._____

7. Do you know, Professor Bullock[ ] where I could find the January issue of the *Journal of Reading?*   7._____

8. Unfortunately, the administration was located in an old[ ] dilapidated[ ] three-story building.   8._____

9. Time having run out[ ] I was obliged to hand in my test paper before I had finished.   9._____

10. Vitamin D may be an important dietary supplement[ ] new studies link Vitamin D to the prevention of breast and colon cancer.   10._____

11. All farmers[ ] who have had their crops destroyed by this year's drought[ ] will be compensated.   11._____

12. Checking his fax machine[ ] Harold discovered that he actually had three important messages.   12._____

13. She had been in the hospital[ ] therefore, she was behind in three classes.   13._____

14. During his first three years of college[ ] he attended three different institutions.   14._____

15. Having eaten Spam as a child[ ] Sam declared that he would never serve it in his home.   15._____

16. Poised and completely at ease[ ] the student-body president greeted the incoming freshmen.   16._____

17. "The answer is here somewhere," Holmes said[ ] "and I am sure we can find it."   17._____

18. Most Americans don't know much about the presidential candidates[ ] sadly, most citizens rely on television ads as their main source of information.   18._____

19. Ms. Vane, the principal, waited[ ] until the students in the assembly hall were quiet.   19._____

20. The mayor adjusted his tie, smiled, and coughed[ ] then he said he was glad that the question had been asked.   20._____

21. Having visited the Rock and Roll Hall of Fame in Cleveland[ ] Sue planned to write a book about Elvis.

21._____

22. When traveling in another country, always pack some routine over-the-counter products[ ] otherwise, you may end up searching for a bottle of aspirin in a foreign drugstore.

22._____

23. Snowshoes are essential for getting around on foot in deep snow[ ] however, they are little use in mild, snowless winters.

23._____

24. This arrangement certainly is the best of all possible worlds[ ] don't you think?

24._____

25. Exercising is really beneficial[ ] because it helps to reduce physical and psychological stress.

25._____

26. After they graduated, they packed their belongings[ ] and moved to a small town in Ohio.

26._____

27. Amy was aware as she raced down the hill[ ] that this event would be her last chance ever to win a medal in the downhill.

27._____

28. He plans to study for his physics exam[ ] write a paper for English[ ] and send an e-mail message to a friend.

28._____

29. Tuberculosis, Dr. Phillips[ ] will be the main focus for my research paper.

29._____

30. Our representatives included Will Leeds, a member of the Rotary Club[ ] Augusta Allcott, a banker[ ] and Bill Rogers, president of the Chamber of Commerce.

30._____

31. Many companies are adding college-tuition assistance programs to their existing benefit packages[ ] and are providing on-site child care.

31._____

32. It turns out that Columbus was not the first European to reach North America[ ] researchers have established the authenticity of a medieval map copied from records left by Norse explorers.

32._____

33. He followed the trail to the summit[ ] later, he found the entrance to the mine.

33._____

34. The computer virus swallowed up the files on my hard drive[ ] and caused me to lose several days' worth of work.

34._____

35. Without seeing where I made my mistakes on my essay[ ] I simply can't hope to do better next time.

35._____

36. Peter lives in Minnesota[ ] Howard, in New York.

36._____

37. Television audiences are demanding[ ] that there be less violence in early evening programs.

37._____

38. His adviser's signature being required[ ] Fred went to the administration building.

38._____

39. Failing to make the right turn on the highway[ ] caused us to arrive two hours late.

39._____

40. Fighting his way through a host of tacklers[ ] he scored a touchdown.

40._____

41. Dead-end jobs[ ] generally to be avoided by younger people[ ] may be perfect for retired senior citizens.

41._____

42. When the family found the tin box of letters from the nineteenth century[ ] they donated the letters to a local university.

42._____

43. Upon graduating from college[ ] he went into the service.

43._____

44. Stock-car racing has steadily increased in popularity[ ] since 1980, attendance at races has more than doubled.

44._____

45. Since the economy seems to be improving[ ] economists predict that consumers will purchase more expensive items such as cars, stereo equipment, and jewelry.

45._____

46. After watching the thriller video[ ] Thelma slept with the lights on for a week.   46. _____

47. Even after thirty years, Giovanni Giacommeti's metal sculptures are still well received by the public[ ] for each statue seems to capture life in the twentieth century.   47. _____

48. Rex was angry with his wife Gail[ ] for having broken many of the commitments listed in their twenty-page prenuptial agreement.   48. _____

49. He asked you to help him with his biology[ ] didn't he?   49. _____

50. They suspected that the leather jacket might be found[ ] if someone were to look through the gym lockers.   50. _____

52. PUNCTUATION: THE APOSTROPHE

(Study 40-42, The Apostrophe)

First, write the number of the **correct** choice (**1** or **2**). Next, write the number (**3** to **6**, from the list below) of the **reason** for your choice. If your choice has no **apostrophe**, write nothing for the second answer.

3. singular possessive   5. contraction
4. plural possessive   6. plural of letter or symbol used as a word

Example: The day is (1)**our's**(2)**ours**.   <u> 2 </u> ____

1. I (1)**didn't** (2)**did'nt** have enough money with me to pay the taxi.   1.____ ____

2. The (1)**Smith's** (2)**Smiths** have planned a murder mystery party.   2.____ ____

3. The (1)**James'** (2)**Jameses** are moving to Seattle.   3.____ ____

4. My (1)**brother-in-law's** (2)**brother's-in-law** medical practice is flourishing.   4.____ ____

5. The (1)**Russo's** (2)**Russos'** new home is spacious.   5.____ ____

6. (1)**Its** (2)**It's** important to exercise several times a week.   6.____ ____

7. (1)**Who's** (2)**Whose** responsible for the increased production of family-oriented movies?   7.____ ____

8. The two (1)**girl's** (2)**girls'** talent was quite evident to everyone.   8.____ ____

9. Soccer has become the new American sport of the (1)**1990s** (2)**1990's**.   9.____ ____

10. It will be a two-(1)**day's** (2)**days'** drive to Galveston.   10.____ ____

11. He went on a one-(1)**week's** (2)**weeks'** trip to Puerto Rico.   11.____ ____

12. Mary accidentally spilled tea on her (1)**bosses** (2)**boss's** report.   12.____ ____

13. After the long absence, they fell into (1)**each others'** (2)**each other's** arms.   13.____ ____

14. Two different women claimed the diamond ring was (1)**her's** (2)**hers**.   14.____ ____

15. Geraldine uses too many (1)**ands** (2)**and's** in most of her presentations.   15.____ ____

16. His (1)**O's** (2)**Os** have a solid black center; his typewriter needs to be cleaned.   16.____ ____

17. (1)**Wer'ent** (2)**Weren't** you surprised by the success of her book?   17.____ ____

18. Which is safer, your van or (1)**ours** (2)**our's**?   18.____ ____

19. Georgiana insisted, "I (1)**have'nt** (2)**haven't** seen Sandy for weeks."   19.____ ____

20. He bought fifty (1)**cents** (2)**cents'** worth of bubblegum.   20.____ ____

21. The back alley was known to be a (1)**thieve's** (2)**thieves'** hangout.   21.____ ____

22. (1)**Paul's and David's** (2)**Paul and David's** senior project was praised by their advisor.   22.____ ____

23. The (1)**children's** (2)**childrens'** kitten ate our goldfish.   23.____ ____

24. "Your (1)**times** (2)**time's** up!" declared Jim, who had been waiting for the treadmill.   24.____ ____

25. The local (1)**coal miner's** (2)**coal miners'** union was the subject of Bill's documentary.   25.____ ____

53. PUNCTUATION: THE APOSTROPHE

(Study 40-42, The Apostrophe)

For each bracketed apostrophe,

Write **1** if the apostrophe is **correct**;
Write **0** if the apostrophe is **incorrect**.

(Use the first column for the first apostrophe in each sentence, use the second column for the second apostrohe.)

Example: **Who[']s** on first? Where's **today[']s** lineup?   <u> 1 </u>   <u> 0 </u>

1. This is no one **else[']s** fault but **your[']s**, I'm sorry to say.   1.____ ____

2. **Mrs. Jackson[']s** invitation to the **William[']s** must have gone astray.   2.____ ____

3. He **would[']nt** know that information after only two **day[']s** employment.   3.____ ____

4. **Wer[']ent** they fortunate that the stolen car wasn't **their[']s**?   4.____ ____

5. **It[']s** a pity that the one bad cabin would be **our[']s**.   5.____ ____

6. **We[']re** expecting the **Wagner[']s** to meet us in Colorado for a ski trip. 6.____ ____

7. "**Where[']s** your driver's license?" was the **officer[']s** first question.   7.____ ____

8. **Does[']nt** the student realize that he **won[']t** be able to take the final early?   8.____ ____

9. The two sisters had agreed that **they']d** stop wearing each **others[']** shoes.   9.____ ____

10. **She[']s** not going to accept **anybody[']s** advice, no matter how sound it may be.   10.____ ____

11. The **students[']** complaints about the **professor[']s** attitude in class were finally addressed by the administration.   11.____ ____

12. **He[']s** hoping for ten **hours[']** work a week in the library.   12.____ ____

13. The idea of a cultural greeting card business was not **our[']s**; it was **Lois[']s**.   13.____ ____

14. There are three **i[']s** in the word *optimistic;* there are two **r[']s** in the word *embarrass.*   14.____ ____

15. The computer printout consisted of a series of **1[']s** and **0[']s**.   15.____ ____

16. Their advisor sent two dozen yellow **rose[']s** to the Women Student **Association[']s** meeting.   16.____ ____

17. I really **did[']nt** expect to see all of the **drivers[']** finish the race.   17.____ ____

18. **Hav[']ent** you heard about the theft at the **Jone[']s** house?   18.____ ____

19. The popular **mens[']** store established in 1923 **was[']nt** able to compete with the large discount stores in the nearby mall.   19.____ ____

20. I'm sure that, if **he[']s** physically able, **he[']ll** be at the volunteer program.   20.____ ____

21. The responsibility for notifying club members is **her[']s** not **our[']s**.   21.____ ____

22. **Can[']t** I persuade you that **you[']re** now ready to move out of the house?   22.____ ____

23. Both **lawyers[']** used hard-hitting **tactic[']s** to explain why their company should not be required to pay damages.   23. ____ ____

24. In the **1980[']s**, **everyones[']** goal was to be personally satisfied.   24. ____ ____

25. My **mother-in-law[']s** books are aimed at a **women[']s** market.   25. ____ ____

54. PUNCTUATION: THE APOSTROPHE

(Study 40-42, The Apostrophe.)

In the paragraph below, every word ending in *s* has a number next to it. In each corresponding blank after the paragraph,

write **1** if the word should end in **'s**;
write **2** if the word should end in **s'**;
Write **0** if the word needs **no apostrophe**.

Example: We took showers_Ex after the game.   Ex. _____0_____

All young performers$_1$ dream of gaining recognition from their audiences$_2$ and of selling millions of copies$_3$

of their work. These were Annie Smiths$_4$ dreams when she left her mother and fathers$_5$ home and ran off to

New York City. At age eighteen, Annie was not prepared for the difficulties$_6$ she faced by living alone and

working in a large city. Her wages$_7$ as a waitress barely covered a months$_8$ rent. And she still needed to buy

groceries$_9$ and pay her utilities.$_{10}$ It took Annie several months$_{11}$ time to find two suitable roommates, who

would share the rent and other bills. However, the roommates$_{12}$ also helped in other important ways, for when

Annie felt that she couldn't go for another audition, her roommates$_{13}$ encouragement to continue helped

bolster Annies$_{14}$ determination. Annie realized that for anyones$_{15}$ dream to happen, a lot of hard work had to

come first.

1. _____   9. _____
2. _____   10. _____
3. _____   11. _____
4. _____   12. _____
5. _____   13. _____
6. _____   14. _____
7. _____   15. _____
8. _____

55. PUNCTUATION: ITALICS

(Study 43, Italics [Underlining])

Write the number of the **reason** for each use of italics:

1. **title of book, magazine, newspaper, or electronic publications**
2. **title of musical production, play, film, or TV show**
3. **name of ship, aircraft, or spacecraft**
4. **title of painting or sculpture**
5. **foreign word not yet Anglicized**
6. **word, letter, figure, or symbol referred to as such**
7. **emphasis**

Example: I read nothing but *TV Guide*.   _____1_____

1. The *Titanic* was thought to be an unsinkable ship.   1._____

2. *Peter Pan* seems to be shown on television every spring.   2._____

3. For many years, the *Manchester Guardian* has been a leading newspaper in England.   3._____

4. While dieting, I couldn't read *Saveur*, my favorite food magazine.   4._____

5. Directions on the test indicated that all questions were to be answered with *1s* or *2s*.   5._____

6. A mnemonic device for helping a student spell the word *principal* is the expression "The *Principal* is your *pal.*"   6._____

7. Susan learned to spell the word *villain* by thinking of a *villa in* Italy.   7._____

8. He decided to subscribe to *Time* or *Newsweek*.   8._____

9. The statue *The Women of Belfast* is on loan from the Ulster Museum.   9._____

10. An article had been written recently about the submarine *Nautilus*.   10._____

11. N. Scott Momaday's *1969: The Way to Rainy Mountain* recounts the Kiowa Indians' migration to the American plains.   11._____

12. How many *s's* and *i's* are there in your last name?   12._____

13. Many television critics feel that the series *Friends* portrays how relationships were formed in the mid-1990s.   13._____

14. The American pronunciation of *vase* is *vas*; the British pronunciation is *vaz*.   14._____

15. Richard Rodriguez's autobiography, *Hunger of Memory*, helped me understand some of the issues surrounding bilingual education.   15._____

16. American women are learning to say *no* to many professional demands so that they have time for family and friends.   16._____

17. Aboard the *Enterprise*, the captain made plans to return to the planet Zircon to rescue Mr. Spock.   17._____

18. He has a leading role in the opera *Pagliacci*, hasn't he?   18._____

19. Children and adults are both fascinated with the software package *Oregon Trail*. 19._____

20. The first American to orbit the earth was John Glenn in *Friendship 7*. 20._____

21. Her printed *R's* and *B's* closely resemble each other. 21._____

22. Although he never held office, Lopez was the *de facto* ruler of his country. 22._____

23. Some people spell and pronounce the words *athlete* and *athletics* as if there were an *e* after *th* in each word. 23._____

24. The movie *A Family Thing* addresses racial issues in the United States in a thought-provoking and sensitive manner. 24._____

25. The original meaning of the word *mad* was "disordered in mind" or "insane." 25._____

Instructions: In each sentence there is a word or group of words that should be italicized. Underline these words, and write in the blank the number (**1** to **7**) of the reasons for the italics:

1. title of book, magazine, newspaper, or electronic publications
2. title of musical production, play, film, or TV show
3. name of ship, aircraft, or spacecraft
4. title of painting or sculpture
5. foreign word not yet Anglicized
6. word, letter, figure, or symbol referred to as such
7. emphasis

Example: We were all on the cover of Newsweek. __1__

1. My favorite album from the 1980s is Trio, which featured Linda Ronstadt, Emmylou Harris, and Dolly Parton. 1._____

2. Deciding to come home by ship, we made reservations on the Queen Elizabeth II. 2._____

3. Geraldine went downtown to buy copies of Esquire and Field and Stream. 3._____

4. "It's time for a change," affirmed the candidate during the debate. 4._____

5. Crazy for You, a revival of a 1930s musical, has done well on Broadway. 5._____

6. The New York Times must have weighed ten pounds last Sunday. 6._____

7. The Mystery Theater series on public television promises amateur sleuths a weekly escape into murder and intrigue. 7._____

8. For my birthday a friend gave me the book Ladder of Years by Ann Tyler. 8._____

9. Among the magazines scattered in the room was a copy of Popular Mechanics. 9._____

10. Maya Angelou's first published work, I Know Why The Caged Bird Sings, is an autobiography describing the first sixteen years of her life. 10._____

11. When I try to pronounce the word statistics, I always stumble over it. 11._____

12. I still have difficulty remembering the difference between continual and continuous. 12._____

13. "There is no such word as alright," said Dr. Williams as she wrote the sentence on the chalkboard. 13._____

14. Picasso's Guernica depicts the horrors of war. 14._____

15. The Thinker is a statue that many people admire. 15._____

16. Spike Lee's Malcolm X inspired me.   16. _____

17. You'll enjoy reading "The Man of the House" in the book Fifty Great Short Stories.   17. _____

18. The British spelling of the word humor is h-u-m-o-u-r.   18. _____

19. "How to Heckle Your Prof" was an essay in John James's How to Get Thrown
    Out of College.   19. _____

20. Michelangelo's Last Judgment shows "the omnipotence of his artistic ability."   20. _____

21. The source of the above quotation is the Encyclopaedia Britannica.   21. _____

22. The fourth opera in this winter's series is Verdi's Don Carlo.   22. _____

23. Her argument was ad hominem.   23. _____

24. Perry won the spelling bee's award for creative expression with his rendition of
    antidisestablishmentarianism.   24. _____

25. The instructor said that Sam's 7s and his 4s look very much alike.   25. _____

56. PUNCTUATION: QUOATATION MARKS

(Study 44-48, Quotation Marks)

Insert quotation marks (double or single, as needed) at the proper places in each sentence. Then, write the number (**1** to **10** from the list below) of the reason for the quotation marks:

1. direct quotation	**6. title of poem**
2. title of chapter	**7. title of song**
3. title of magazine article	**8. title of newspaper article or editorial**
4. title of short story	**9. definition**
5. title of essay	**10. nickname**

Example: My childhood nickname Stringbean no longer fits me.   <u> 10 </u>

1. The article about silk, The Queen of Textiles, appeared in *National Geographic* magazine in January 1984.   1._____

2. Murder in the Rain Forest, which appeared in *Time* magazine, told of the death of a courageous Brazilian environmentalist.   2._____

3. W.C. Fields's dying words were I'd rather be in Philadelphia.   3._____

4. The poem The Swing was written by Robert Louis Stevenson.   4._____

5. Be prepared, warned the weather forecaster, for a particularly harsh winter this year.   5._____

6. Childhood Memories is a chapter in the reader *Growing Up in the South*.   6._____

7. In the magazine *Arizona Highways*, Joyce Muench described the unusual cloud formations that enhance Arizona's scenery in Kingdom of the Skies.   7._____

8. The word *cavalier* was originally defined as a man on a horse.   8._____

9. James Rocket Man Hamilton spoke to the members of the football team.   9._____

10. One of my favorite short stories is Eudora Welty's A Worn Path.   10._____

11. The song The Wind Beneath My Wings was sung to inspire mentors to stay with the literary program.   11._____

12. The World is Too Much with Us is a poem by William Wordsworth.   12._____

13. The New Order is an article that appeared in *Time* magazine.   13._____

14. An article that appeared in the *Washington Post* is Can We Abolish Poverty?   14._____

15. Cousins' essay The Right to Die poses the question of whether suicide is ever an acceptable response to life circumstances.   15._____

16. The Love Song of J. Alfred Prufrock is a poem by T. S. Eliot.   16._____

17. Under the Stars is a poem written by Tess Gallagher.   17._____

18. The concluding song of the evening was Auld Lang Syne.   18._____

19. We read a poem by Alice Walker entitled Women.   19._____

20. Police Chief Busted is the title of an editorial in the *Wall Street Journal*.   20._____

21. Tom had private tutoring from Ezell The Disk Man Adams.   21._____

22. We read Octavio Paz's essay The Day of the Dead.   22._____

23. She read Julio Cortazar's short story The Health of the Sick.   23._____

24. *Discography* means a comprehensive list of recordings made by a particular
    performer or of a particular composer's work.   24._____

57. PUNCTUATION: QUOTATION MARKS

(Study 44-48, Quotation Marks)

Write **1** if the punctuation in brackets is **correct**.
Write **0** if it is **incorrect**.

Example: "Want to play ball, Scarecrow[?]" the Wicked Witch asked, a ball of fire in her hand.   1. ____1____

1. The late arrivals asked[,"]When did the party end?"   1. _____

2. When the job was finished, the worker asked, "How do you like it[?"]   2. _____

3. In the first semester we read Gabriel García Márquez's short story "Big Mama's Funeral["].   3. _____

4. "Where are you presently employed?["] the interviewer asked.   4. _____

5. "When you finish your rough draft," said Professor Grill,"] send it to my e-mail address."   5. _____

6. Who was it who mused, "Where are the snows of yesteryear["?]   6. _____

7. Dr. Nelson, our anthropology teacher, asked, "How many of you have read *The Autobiography of Malcolm X* [?"]   7. _____

8. "We need more study rooms in the library[,"] declared one presidential candidate in the student government debate.   8. _____

9. "Write when you can[,"] Mother said as I left for the airport.   9. _____

10. To *dissuade* means "to persuade someone not to do something[."]   10. _____

11. "Ask not what your country can do for you[;"] ask what you can do for your country."   11. _____

12. "Our language creates problems when we talk about race in America.["] ["]We don't have enough terms to explain the complexities of cultural diversity."   12. _____

13. "Do you remember Father's saying, 'Never give up['?"] she asked.   13. _____

14. She began reciting the opening lines of one of Elizabeth Barrett Browning's sonnets: "How do I love thee? / Let me count the ways[."]   14. _____

15. Gwendolyn Brooks's poem ["]The Bean Eaters["] is one of her best.   15. _____

16. ["]*The Fantasticks*["] is the longest-running musical play in American theater.   16. _____

17. Annette sighed, "Don't you get tired of hearing karaoke performers butcher 'Unchained Melody[?'"]   17. _____

18. "Shall I read aloud Whitman's poem 'Out of the Cradle Endlessly Rocking['?"] she asked.   18. _____

19. Have you read Adrienne Rich's poem "Necessities of Life[?"]   19. _____

20. When Susan saw the show about America's homeless, she exclaimed, "I have to find a way to help[!"]   20. _____

21. The noun *neurotic* is defined as "an emotionally unstable individual["].   21. _____

22. "I'm going to the newsstand," he said[, "]for a copy of the Atlantic."   22._____

23. "Do you believe in fairies[?"] Peter Pan asks the children.   23._____

24. How maddening of her to reply calmly, "You're so right["!]   24._____

25. "Come as soon as you can," said Mother to the plumber[. "]The basement is already flooded."   25._____

26. My best composition this semester was entitled "The Reason I Decided to Become an English Major[."]   26._____

27. "The Lottery[,"] a short story by Shirley Jackson, was discussed in Janet's English class.   27._____

28. The reporter said[, "]Thank you for the lead on the story," and ran off to trace down the source.   28._____

29. "Was the treaty signed in 1815[?"] the professor asked, "or in 1814?"   29._____

30. The mayor said, "I guarantee that urban renewal will move forward rapidly[;"] however, I don't believe him.   30._____

31. Richard Rodriguez writes: "Only when I was able to think of myself as an American, no longer an alien in *gringo* society, could I seek the rights and opportunities necessary for full public individuality["·]   31._____

32. "Have you seen the rough draft of the article?" asked Jackie[?]   32._____

33. I reread E.B. White's "The Ring of Time ["·]   33._____

58. PUNCTUATION: ITALICS AND QUOTATION MARKS

(Study 43, Italics; and 44-48, Quotation Marks)

Write the number of the correct choice.

Example: A revival of Cole Porter's play (1)*Anything Goes* (2)"Anything Goes" is playing at the Beaumont Theatre.

_____1_____

1. (1)"Cats," (2)*Cats*, which is one of Broadway's most successful plays, is based on the work of T.S. Eliot.

1._____

2. An editorial titled (1)*Public Transit Needs Public Money* (2)"Public Transit Needs Public Money" appeared in the *New York Times*.

2._____

3. (1)"London Bridge" (2)*London Bridge* is a popular nursery rhyme.

3._____

4. Paul Kennedy's book (1)*The Rise and Fall of Great Powers* (2)"The Rise and Fall of the Great Powers" discusses how nations become politically and militarily dominant.

4._____

5. The title of the *Psychology Today* article is (1)*Child Complaints* (2)"Child Complaints."

5._____

6. The closing song of the concert was (1)"R-e-s-p-e-c-t" (2)*R-e-s-p-e-c-t*.

6._____

7. (1)*A Haunted House* (2)"A Haunted House" is a short story by Virginia Woolf.

7._____

8. The brevity of Carl Sandburg's poem (1)*Fog* (2)"Fog" appealed to her.

8._____

9. Jack received (1)*A's* (2) "A's" in three of his classes this fall.

9._____

10. She used too many (1)*and's* (2)"and's" in her introductory speech.

10._____

11. (1)*Science and Religion* (2)"Science and Religion" is an essay by Albert Einstein.

11._____

12. He has purchased tickets for the opera (1)"Faust" (2)*Faust*.

12._____

13. Sharon didn't use a spell-check program and, therefore, unfortunately misspelled (1)*psychology* (2)"psychology" throughout her paper.

13._____

14. Dr. Baylor spent two classes on Wallace Stevens's poem (1)"The Idea of Order At Key West" (2)*The Idea of Order at Key West*.

14._____

15. His favorite newspaper has always been the (1)*Times* (2)"Times."

15._____

16. (1)"Our Town" (2)*Our Town* is a play by Thornton Wilder.

16._____

17. The word altogether means (1)"wholly" or "thoroughly" (2)*wholly* or *thoroughly*.

17._____

18. (1)*What Women Want* (2)"What Women Want" is an essay by Margaret Mead.

18._____

19. James Thurber's short story (1)The Secret Life of Walter Mitty (2)"The Secret Life of Walter Mitty" amused her.

19._____

20. The Players' Guild will produce Marlowe's (1)*Dr. Faustus* (2)"Dr. Faustus" next month.

20._____

21. Helen Cook's article (1)*Reading for Pleasure* (2)"Reading for Pleasure" appeared in the January 1996 edition of the *Journal of Reading*.

21._____

22. (1)*Biology: Science of Life* (2)"Biology: Science of Life" is our very expensive textbook for biochemistry class.

22._____

23. One of the first assignments for our African American history classes was James Baldwin's book (1)*Notes of a Native Son* (2)"Notes of a Native Son."

23. _____

24. Our film class saw Truffaut's (1)*Shoot the Piano Player* (2)"Shoot the Piano Player" last week.

24. _____

25. She read (1)*Dover Beach,* (2)"Dover Beach," a poem by Matthew Arnold.

25. _____

26. (1)*Pygmalion* (2)"Pygmalion" is a play by George Bernard Shaw.

26. _____

27. You fail to distinguish between the words (1)*range* and *vary* (2)"range" and "vary."

27. _____

28. I read a poem by Yeats titled (1)"The Cat and the Moon" (2) *The Cat and the Moon.*

28. _____

29. Madeline decided to treat herself by ordering a subscription to (1)*Time* (2)"Time."

29. _____

30. (1)*Fragmented* (2)"Fragmented" is a play by my colleague Prester Pickett.

30. _____

31. I used (1) "Do Lie Detectors Lie?" (2)*Do Lie Detectors Lie?* from *Science* to write my report on famous murder trials.

31. _____

32. Through Kevin Coyne's book (1)"A Day in the Night of America," (2)*A Day in the Night of America*, readers have a chance to see how 7.3 million Americans spend their time working a night shift.

32. _____

33. Virginia Woolf's essay (1)"Professions for Women" (2)*Professions for Women* was first delivered as a speech to a group of upper-class women who were just beginning careers.

33. _____

59. PUNCTUATION: THE COLON, THE DASH, PARENTHESE, AND BRACKETS

(Study 49-50, The Colon; 51, The Dash; 52-53, Parentheses; and 54, Brackets)

Write **1** if the colon is used **correctly**.
Write **0** if it is used **incorrectly**.

Example: We invited: Larry, Moe, and Curly.   0

1. Casey's first question was: Can anybody here play this game?   1. _____

2. The coach signaled the strategy: we would try a double steal on the next pitch.   2. _____

3. Dear Sir: My five years' experience as a high school English teacher qualifies me to be the editor of your newsletter.   3. _____

4. Dear "Stretch": The whole group—all eight of us—plans to spend the weekend with you.   4. _____

5. Laurie's shopping list included these items: truffles, caviar, champagne, and a dozen hot dogs.   5. _____

6. The carpenter brought his: saw, hammer, square, measuring tape, and nails.   6. _____

7. College students generally complain about: their professors, the cafeteria food, and their roommates.   7. _____

8. She began her letter to Tom with these words: "I'll love you forever!"   8. _____

9. Her train reservations were for Tuesday at 3:30 p.m.   9. _____

10. The dean demanded that: the coaches, the players, and the training staff meet with him immediately.   10. _____

11. Tonight's winning numbers are: 169, 534, and 086.   11. _____

12. She was warned that the project would require two qualities: creativity and perseverance.   12. _____

13. The project has been delayed: the chairperson has been hospitalized because of emergency surgery.   13. _____

14. The president of the university declared: "The Smith Building, the oldest structure on campus, will be rebuilt despite extensive fire damage."   14. _____

15. I packed my backpack with: bubble bath, a couple of novels, and some comfortable clothes.   15. _____

The Dash, Parentheses, and Brackets

Set off the boldface words by inserting the **correct** punctuation.
Then write the number of the punctuation you inserted:

1. dash(es) 2. parentheses 3. brackets

Example: Senator Aikin **Rep. Maine** voted for the proposal.   <u>   2   </u>

1. My new car **oh, when would I ever be able to afford a new car!**   1. _____

2. Holmes had deduced **who knew how?** that the man had been born on a moving train during the rainy season. [Punctuate to indicate a sharp interruption.]   2. _____

3. He will be considered for **this is between you and me, of course** one of the three vice-presidencies in the firm. [Punctuate to indicate merely incidental comment.]   3. _____

4. I simply told her **and I'm glad I did!** that I would never set foot in her house again. [Punctuate to indicate merely incidental comment.]   4. _____

5. Campbell's work on *Juvenal* **see reference** is an excellent place to start.   5. _____

6. At Yosemite National Park we watched the feeding of the bears **from a safe distance, you can be sure**. [Punctuate to achieve a dramatic effect.]   6. _____

7. Her essay was entitled "The American Medical System and It's **sic** Problems."   7. _____

8. The rules for using parentheses **see page 7** are not easy to understand.   8. _____

9. Only one thing stood in the way of buying a sailboat **credit**.   9. _____

10. The statement read: "Enclosed you will find one hundred dollars **$100** to cover damages."   10. _____

11. David liked one kind of dessert **apple pie**.   11. _____

12. **Eat, drink, and be merry** gosh, I can hardly wait for senior week.   12. _____

13. The essay begins: "For more than a hundred years **from 1337 until 1453** the British and French fought a pointless war." [Punctuate to show that the boldface expression is inserted editorially.]   13. _____

14. The concert begins at **by the way, when does the concert begin**?   14. _____

15. Getting to work at eight o'clock every morning **I don't have to remind you how much I dislike getting up early** seemed almost more than I cared to undertake. [Punctuate to indicate merely incidental comment.]   15. _____

16. She said, "Two of my friends **one has really serious emotional problems** need psychiatric help." [Punctuate to achieve a dramatic effect.]   16. _____

17. Within the last year, I have received three **or was it four?** letters from her. [Punctuate to indicate merely incidental comment.]   17. _____

18. Julius was born in 1900 **?** and came west as a young boy.   18. _____

60. PUNCTUATION: HYPHEN

(Study 55, The Hyphen)

Write **1** if the use or omission of a hyphen is **correct**.
Write **0** if it is **incorrect**.

Example: Seventy six trombones led the big parade.   ___0___

1. Dana made a **semi-serious** effort to pick up the check.   1._____

2. "I **c-c-can't** breathe because of my asthma," panted the patient.   2._____

3. The **eleven-year-old** girl planned to be an astronaut.   3._____

4. She rented a **two room** apartment close to campus.   4._____

5. The speaker was **well known** to everyone connected with administration.   5._____

6. The **well-known** author was autographing his latest novel in the bookstore today. 6._____

7. The team averaged over **fifty-thousand** spectators a game.   7._____

8. The contractor expects to build many **five-** and **six-room** houses this year.   8._____

9. The senator composed a **carefully-worded** statement for a press conference.   9._____

10. I sent in my subscription to a new **bi-monthly** magazine.   10._____

11. Sam's **brother-in-law** delighted in teasing his sister by belching at family dinners. 11._____

12. At last her dream of an **up to date** kitchen was coming true.   12._____

13. He made every effort to **recover** the missing gems.   13._____

14. Because she spilled coffee on her paper, she had to **re-write** the final copy.   14._____

15. At **eighty-four**, Hartley still rides his motorcycle in the mountains on sunny days. 15._____

16. Charles will run in the **hundred yard** dash next Saturday.   16._____

17. "The children are not to have any more **c-a-n-d-y**," said Mother.   17._____

18. After he graduated from college, he became a manager of the **student-owned**
    bookstore.   18._____

19. The idea of a **thirty hour** week appealed to the workers.   19._____

20. Baird played **semi-professional** baseball before going into the major leagues.   20._____

21. Customers began avoiding the **hot-tempered** clerk in the shoe department.   21._____

22. Al's main problem is that he lacked **self-confidence**.   22._____

23. The **brand-new** vacuum cleaner made a loud squealing noise every time we
    turned it on.   23._____

24. The word processing software was **brand new**.   24._____

25. Mr. Pollard's major research interest was **seventeenth-century** French history.   25._____

61. PUNCTUATION: REVIEW

(Study 30-55, Punctuation)

Write **1** for each statement that is **true**.
Write **0** for each that is **false**.

Example: A **period** is used at the end of a declarative statement.   _____1_____

1. **Single quotation marks** are used to enclose a quotation within a quotation.   1._____
2. An **apostrophe** is used to indicate the possessive case of personal pronouns.   2._____
3. The **question mark** is always placed inside closing quotation marks.   3._____
4. A **dash** may be indicated by the use of two hyphens on the word processor or typewriter.   4._____
5. A **dash** is used before the author's name following a direct quotation.   5._____
6. **Parentheses** are used to enclose editorial remarks in a direct quotation.   6._____
7. **Commas** are **not** used to set off a restrictive adjective clause.   7._____
8. A **semicolon** is used to set off an absolute phrase from the rest of the sentence.   8._____
9. The use of **brackets** around the word *sic* indicates an error occurring in quoted material.   9._____
10. Mild interjections should be followed by an **exclamation point**; strong ones, by a **comma**.   10._____
11. An indirect question is followed by a **period**.   11._____
12. A **semicolon** is used after the expression Dear Sir.   12._____
13. The title of a magazine article should be underlined to designate the use of **italics**.   13._____
14. **Ms**. may take a period but **Miss** does not.   14._____
15. The title of a newspaper is enclosed in **double quotation marks**.   15._____
16. **Mr. Jone's, Mr. Jones'**, and **Mr. Jones's** are all acceptable possessive forms of *Mr. Jones*.   16._____
17. The title at the head of a composition should be enclosed in **double quotation marks**.   17._____
18. **No apostrophe** is needed in the following greeting: "Merry Christmas from the Palmers."   18._____
19. The **possessive** of *somebody else* is *somebody's else*.   19._____
20. The **possessive** of *mother-in-law* is *mother's-in-law*.   20._____
21. A **semicolon** is used between two independent clauses joined by **and** if one or both clauses contain internal commas.   21._____
22. A quotation consisting of several sentences takes **double quotation marks** at the beginning of the first sentence and at the end of the last sentence.   22._____

23. A quotation consisting of several paragraphs takes **double quotation marks** at the beginning and end of each paragraph.

23._____

24. The **plurals** of letters are formed by the addition of 's to the singular form.

24._____

25. The word *the* is **italicized** in the name of a newspaper or a magazine.

25._____

26. A polite request in the form of a question is followed by a **period**.

26._____

27. **Single quotation marks** may be substituted for double quotation marks around any quoted passage.

27._____

28. The **comma** is always placed **outside** quotation marks.

28._____

29. The **colon** and **semicolon** are always placed inside quotation marks.

29._____

30. A **comma** is always used to separate the two parts of a compound predicate.

30._____

31. The expression **such as** is always followed by a **comma**.

31._____

32. The **nonsentence** is a legitimate unit of expression and may be followed by a **period**.

32._____

33. When a declarative sentence ends with a confirmatory question, a **comma** is used between them.

33._____

34. **Parentheses** are used around words that are to be deleted from a manuscript.

34._____

35. A **comma** is used between two independent clauses not joined by a coordinating conjunction.

35._____

36. A **semicolon** is used after the salutation of a business letter.

36._____

37. The subject of a sentence should be separated from the predicate by use of a **comma**.

37._____

38. An overuse of **underlining** (italics) for emphasis should be avoided.

38._____

39. The **contraction** of the words **have not** is written thus: **hav'ent**.

39._____

40. Nonrestrictive clauses are always set off with **commas**.

40._____

41. **Double quotation marks** are used around the name of a ship.

41._____

42. A **comma** is used before the word *then* when it introduces a second clause.

42._____

43. The prefix *semi* always requires a **hyphen**.

43._____

44. **No comma** is required in the following sentence: "Where do you wish to go?" he asked.

44._____

45. A **dash** is a legitimate substitute for all other marks of punctuation.

45._____

46. A **slash** is used to separate two lines of poetry quoted in a running text.

46._____

47. A **dash** is placed between nouns used as alternatives.

47._____

48. Every introductory prepositional phrase is set off by a **comma**.

48._____

49. An introductory adverbial clause is usually set off with a **comma**.

49._____

50. A **colon** may be used instead of a **semicolon** between two independent clauses when the second clause is an explanation of the first.

50._____

62. REVIEW: PUNCTUATION

(Study 30-55, Punctuation)

Write **1** if the punctuation in brackets is **correct**.
Write **0** if it is **incorrect**. (Use only one number in each blank.)

Example: The church bells [,] have been ringing all morning.   ___0___

1. He found math difficult[;] but, because he worked so hard, he earned a B.   1._____

2. The Messicks were late[,] their car battery having gone dead.   2._____

3. I wondered why we couldn't get rid of the computer virus[?]   3._____

4. Dear Dr. Stanley[;] Thank you for your letter of May 10.   4._____

5. Rafael enjoyed inviting his friends[,] and preparing elaborate meals for them; however, most of his attempts were disasters.   5._____

6. When the benefits officer described the new medical insurance package, everyone asked, "How much will this new policy cost us["?]   6._____

7. I remembered the job counselor's remark: "If you send out 300 inquiry letters in your hometown without even one response, relocate[."]   7._____

8. "Despite the recession," explained the placement counselor[,] "health-care, construction, and business services still promise an increase in employment opportunities."   8._____

9. A novella by Conrad, a short story by Lawrence, and some poems of Yeats[,] were all assigned for the last week of the semester.   9._____

10. We spent our vacation in Gettysburg, Pennsylvania[,] last August.   10._____

11. Why is it that other children seem to behave better than our[']s?   11._____

12. The relief workers specifically requested food, blankets, and children['s] clothing.   12._____

13. Approximately seven million Americans visit their doctor each year[;] seeking an answer for why they feel so tired.   13._____

14. Whenever he speaks, he's inclined to use too many and-uh[']s between sentences.   14._____

15. The auditor requested[:] to review the medical receipts, our childcare expenses, and any deductions for home improvement.   15._____

16. The last employee to leave the office is responsible for the following[,] turning off the machines, extinguishing all lights, and locking all executives' office doors.   16._____

17. Everywhere there were crowds shouting anti[-]American slogans.   17._____

18. Private colleges and universities are concerned about dwindling enrollment[;] because their tuition costs continue to climb while requests for substantial financial aid are also increasing.   18._____

19. During the whole wretched ordeal of his doctoral exams[;] Charles remained outwardly calm.   19._____

20. More than twenty minutes were cut from the original version of the film[,] the producers told neither the director or the writer.   20. _____

21. The mock epic poem "Casey at the Bat" was first published June 3, 1888[,] in the *Examiner*.   21. _____

22. The fugitive was located near Butte, Montana[,] in a deserted farmhouse.   22. _____

23. The temperature sinking fast as dusk approached[;] we decided to seek shelter for the night.   23. _____

24. By the year 2000, only about half of Americans entering the workforce will be native-born and of European stock[;] thus this country is truly becoming a multiracial society.   24. _____

25. My only cousin[,] who is in the U.S. Air Force[,] is stationed in the Arctic.   25. _____

26. Any U.S. Air Force officer[,] who is stationed in the Arctic[,] receives extra pay.   26. _____

27. Hey! Did you find a biology book in this classroom[?!]   27. _____

28. Charles Goodyear, the man who gave the world vulcanized rubber, personified the qualities of the classic American inventor[:] he spent nine years experimenting to find a waterproof rubber that would be resistant to extreme temperatures.   28. _____

29. Murphy's boss commended him on his frankness and spunk[;] then he fired Murphy.   29. _____

30. The first well-known grocery store group was[,] the Atlantic and Pacific Tea Company, founded in 1859.   30. _____

31. Fernando jumped and squealed with delight[,] because he found a new pair of roller blades under his bed as a present from his family's Three Kings celebration.   31. _____

32. The movies[,] that I prefer to see[,] always have happy endings.   32. _____

33. At the Powwow[;] Anna and her friends entered the Fancy Shawl Dance competition, for they wanted to dance in their new dresses and moccasins.   33. _____

63. MECHANICS: CAPITALS

(Study 61-63, Capitalization)

Write **1** if the boldface words are **correct** in use or omission of capital letters.
Write **0** if they are **incorrect**.

Example: Cajuns speak a dialect of **french**.   0

1. They met at the North Side **Jewish** Center.   1.____

2. My brother teaches **high school**.   2.____

3. The **turkish** bath is closed.   3.____

4. Hyeon Woo's uncle is a Buddhist **Monk**.   4.____

5. When will **Congress** convene?   5.____

6. She is a **Junior** at the University of Houston.   6.____

7. My **daughter** graduated from the University of New Mexico.   7.____

8. He always disliked **Calculus**.   8.____

9. Joe constantly reads about the **Civil War.**   9.____

10. I made an appointment with **Professor** Allen.   10.____

11. She met three **Professors** today.   11.____

12. "Did you save your paper on the disk?" **she** asked.   12.____

13. Each **Spring** I try a new sport.   13.____

14. The deaths were reported in the *Times*.   14.____

15. I worked in the **Southwest**.   15.____

16. Her **Aunt Miriam** has returned.   16.____

17. He's late for his **anthropology** class.   17.____

18. John was **Secretary** of his class.   18.____

19. Woods was promoted to **Major**.   19.____

20. My **Grandfather** wrote to me.   20.____

21. I enrolled in **english** and physics.   21.____

22. He began his letter with "My **Dear** Mrs. Johnson."   22.____

23. He ended it with "Yours **Truly**."   23.____

24. We once lived in the **Northwest**.   24.____

25. I passed German but failed **Biology**.   25.____

26. He entered **College** last fall.   26.____

27. Harold believes there is life on **venus**.   27.____

28. I asked **Mother** for some legal advice.   28.____

29. He goes to **Roosevelt** High School.   29.____

30. Has the **senate** elected a majority leader yet?   30.____

31. My son is now a **Junior**.   31.____

32. I listen to **wfbg** every morning.   32.____

33. We are planning a picnic on Memorial **day**.   33.____

34. I spent the fall break with my **Aunt**.   34.____

35. Her favorite subject is **German**.   35.____

36. The tourists visited **Niagara Falls**.   36.____

37. The **President's** veto of the most recent bill has angered Congress.   37.____

38. He enrolled in **Physics 2**.   38.____

39. This is the **Lutheran Church**.   39.____

40. I am writing a book; **My** editor wants the first chapter soon.   40.____

41. This is *Not* my idea of fun.   41.____

42. I think **mother nature** was particularly cruel this winter.   42.____

43. She earned a **Ph.D.** degree.   43.____

44. The **Championship Fight** was a disappointment.   44.____

45. She declared that charity is considered a **Christian** value.   45.____

46. His father fought in the Korean **war**.   46.____

47. The chairperson of the **Department of History** is Dr. Mo.   47.____

48. He said simply, "**my** name is Bond."   48.____

49. **"Sexual Harassment: The Price of Silence"** is a chapter from my composition reader.   49.____

50. She spent her **Thanksgiving** vacation in Iowa with her family.   50.____

Name _____ Class _____ Date _____ Score (R_____ x 5)_____

64. MECHANICS: CAPITALS

(Study 61-63, Capitalization)

In the first column, write the number of the first correct choice (**1 or 2**).
In the second column, write the number of the second correct choice (**3 or 4**).

Example: Wandering (1)**West** (2)**west**, Max met (3)**Milly** (4)**milly.**   <u>2</u> <u>3</u>

1. Macy's Department (1)**Store** (2)**store** is having a great sale on Italian (3)**Shoes** (4)**shoes.**   1.____ ____

2. Her (1)**Father** (2)**father** went (3)**South** (4)**south** on business.   2.____ ____

3. The new (1)**College** (2)**college** is seeking a (3)**Dean** (4)**dean.**   3.____ ____

4. Children are taught to begin letters with "My (1)**Dear** (2)**dear** (3)**Sir** (4)**sir.**"   4.____ ____

5. Business letters often end with "Very (1)**Truly** (2)**truly** (3)**Yours** (4)**yours.**"   5.____ ____

6. After (1)**Church** (2)**church**, we walked across the Brooklyn (3)**Bridge** (4)**bridge.**   6.____ ____

7. The (1)**Politician** (2)**politician** declared that the protester was (3)**Un-American** (4)**un-American.**   7.____ ____

8. The young (1)**Lieutenant** (2)**lieutenant** prayed to the (3)**Lord** (4)**lord** for courage in the coming battle.   8.____ ____

9. My (1)**Cousin** (2)**cousin** now lives in the (3)**East** (4)**east.**   9.____ ____

10. The (1)**President** (2)**president** addresses (3)**Congress** (4)**congress** tomorrow.   10.____ ____

11. Joan Bailey, (1)**M.D.** (2)**m.d.**, once taught (3)**Biology** (4)**biology.**   11.____ ____

12. Dr. Smith, (1)**Professor** (2)**professor** of (3)**English** (4)**english**, is writing a murder mystery.   12.____ ____

13. The (1)**Comet** (2)**comet** can be seen just below (1)**The Big Dipper** (4)**the Big Dipper.** 13.____ ____

14. "I'm also a graduate of North Harris (1)**College** (2)**college**," (3)**She** (4)**she** added.   14.____ ____

15. The pastor of St. Peter's (1)**Church** (2)**church** is an (3)**Australian** (4)**australian.**   15.____ ____

16. Vera disagreed with the review of "(1)**The** (2)**the** War Chronicles" in (3)**The** (4)**the** *New York Times*.   16.____ ____

17. The club (1)**Treasurer** (2)**treasurer** said that the financial report was "(3)**Almost** (4)**almost** complete."   17.____ ____

18. The (1)**Girl Scout** (2)**girl scout** leader pointed out the (3)**Milky Way** (4)**milky way** to her troop.   18.____ ____

19. Students were required to have the textbook Writing (1)**For** (2)**for** Audience (3)**And** (4)**and** Purpose.   19.____ ____

20. Educational Support Services is in (1)**Room** (2)**room** 110 of Yost (3)**Hall** (4)**hall.**   20.____ ____

153

65. MECHANICS: NUMBERS AND ABBREVIATIONS

(Study 65-67, Numbers, and 68-69, Abbreviations)

Write the number of the **correct** choice.

Example: That book is (1)**3** (2)**three** days overdue.   ____2____

1. (1)**1968** (2)**The year 1968** will be remembered as a turbulent time in the United States.   1._____

2. Several states have raised the drinking age to (1)**twenty-one** (2)**21.**   2._____

3. (1)**Prof.** (2)**Professor** Hilton teaches Asian philosophy.   3._____

4. Lincoln was born in (1)**Ky.** (2)**Kentucky.**   4._____

5. Builders are still reluctant to have a (1)**thirteenth** (2)**13th** floor in any new buildings.   5._____

6. The exam will be held at noon on (1)**Fri.** (2)**Friday.**   6._____

7. The (1)**P.O.** (2)**post office** on campus always has a long line of international
    students mailing letters and packages to their friends and families.   7._____

8. Judd has an interview with the Sherwin Williams (1)**Co.** (2)**Company.**   8._____

9. Nicole will study in Germany, (1)**Eng.** (2)**England**, and Sweden next year.   9._____

10. Evan Booster, (1)**M.D.**, (2)**medical doctor,** is my physician.   10._____

11. Frank jumped 22 feet, (1)**3** (2)**three** inches at the Saturday meet.   11._____

12. For the lab, the department purchased permanent markers, legal pads,
    pencils, (1)**etc.** (2)**and other office supplies.**   12._____

13. For (1)**Xmas** (2)**Christmas**, the Fords planned a quiet family gathering rather than
    their usual ski holiday.   13._____

14. Travis needed to leave for work at exactly 8:00 (1)**a.m.** (2)**o'clock.**   14._____

15. John's stipend was (1)**$2,145** (2)**two thousand one hundred forty-five dollars.**   15._____

16. She will graduate from medical school June (1)**2,** (2)**second**, 1998.   16._____

17. He and his family moved to Vermont last (1)**Feb.** (2)**February**, didn't they?   17._____

18. Over (1)**900** (2)**nine hundred** students attend Roosevelt Junior High School.   18._____

19. Brad loved all of his (1)**phys. ed.** (2)**physical education** electives.   19._____

20. Next year, the convention will be held on April (1)**19,** (2)**19th,** (3)**nineteenth,**
    in Burlington.   20._____

21. The petition contained (1)**2,983** (2)**two thousand nine hundred eighty-three
    names.**   21._____

22. The lottery prize has reached an astonishing (1)**twenty-four million dollars**
    (2)**$24 million.**   22._____

23. The family next door adopted a (1)**two-month-old** (2)**2-month-old** baby girl from
    China.   23._____

24. We had an opportunity to meet (1)**Sen.** (2)**Senator** Lester at the convention.

24. _____

25. The diagram was on (1)**pg.** (2)**page** 44.

25. _____

26. One of my friends will do her student teaching in (1)**TX.** (2)**Texas** this spring.

26. _____

27. When we offered tickets to a baseball game for our raffle, we had (1)**one-third** (2)**1/3rd** of the employees purchase tickets.

27. _____

28. Jack's dissertation was (1)**two hundred fifty** (2)**250** pages.

28. _____

29. The plane expected from (1)**LA early this a.m.** (2)**Los Angeles early this morning is** late.

29. _____

30. The bus arrives at 10:55 a.m. and leaves at (1)**11:00 a.m.** (2)**eleven a.m.**

30. _____

31. Ben earned (1)**three hundred dollars,** (2)**$300,** saved $80, and spent the rest on books and movies.

31. _____

32. Rachel's name was (1)**twenty-sixth** (2)**26th** on the list of high school graduates.

32. _____

33. I need a (1)**4-** (2)**four-**wheel drive vehicle to visit my Uncle Thomas, who lives in a secluded cabin on top of a mountain.

33. _____

66. MECHANICS: CAPITALS, NUMBERS, AND ABBREVIATIONS

(Study 61-63, Capitalization; 65-67, Numbers; and 68-69, Abbreviations)

Write the number of the first **correct** choice (**1** or **2**).
Then write the number of the second **correct** choice (**3** or **4**).

Example: There are only (1)**three** (2)**3** more days until (3)**Summer** (4)**summer** vacation.
    <u> 1 </u> <u> 4 </u>

1. Many of my African-American colleagues have commented that (1)**White** (2)**white** Americans still don't understand the importance of the (3)**Civil Rights Act** (4)**civil rights act** to American culture.
1.____ ____

2. We have an (1)**Aborigine** (2)**aborigine** from Australia studying (3) **Engineering** (4)**engineering** here.
2.____ ____

3. My (1)**Supervisor** (2)**supervisor** said our presentation was (3)**"Insightful!"** (4)**"insightful."**
3.____ ____

4. "I expect," he said, (1)**"To** (2)**"to** get an A in my (3)**Chem.** (4)**chemistry** class."
4.____ ____

5. On June (1)**6,** (2)**6th,** 1995, she spoke at St. Paul's (3)**High School** (4)**high school.**
5.____ ____

6. The new college (1)**President** (2)**president** greeted the (3)**Alumni** (4)**alumni** during the graduation ceremonies.
6.____ ____

7. An (1)**american** (2)**American** flag flies from the top of the Empire State (3)**building** (4)**Building.**
7.____ ____

8. The (1)**treasurer** (2)**Treasurer** of the (3)**Junior Accountants Club** (4)**junior accountants club** has absconded with our dues.
8.____ ____

9. (1)**308** (2)**Three hundred eight** students passed the test out of (3)**427** (4)**four hundred twenty-seven** who took it.
9.____ ____

10. She likes her (1)**english** (2)**English** and (3)**science** (4)**Science** classes.
10.____ ____

11. I soon realized that (1)**spring** (2)**Spring** means rain, rain, and more rain in northeastern (3)**Ohio** (4)**ohio.**
11.____ ____

12. Industry in the (1)**South** (2)**south** is described in this month's (3)*Fortune* (4)*fortune* magazine.
12.____ ____

13. Victor is going to take an (1)**english** (2)**English** course this semester instead of one in (3)**History** (4)**history.**
13.____ ____

14. She was happy; (1)**She** (2)**she** had reservations on (3)**American airlines** (4)**American Airlines.**
14.____ ____

15. The new (1)**doctor** (2)**Doctor** has opened an office on Main (3)**Street** (4)**street.**
15.____ ____

16. The (1)**korean** (2)**Korean** students have planned their (3)**3rd** (4)**third** annual International Dinner.
16.____ ____

17. I spent (1)**New Year's Day** (2)**new year's day** with (3)**mother** (4)**Mother.**
17.____ ____

18. Her (1)**Japanese** (2)**japanese** instructor is touring the (3)**Orient** (4)**orient** over the summer.
18.____ ____

19. I need a (1)**Psychology** (2)**psychology** book from the (3)**Library** (4)**library**.   19. ____ ____

20. The (1)**class** (2)**Class** of '75 honored the (3)**Dean of Men** (4)**dean of men.**   20. ____ ____

21. Leslie enrolled in (1)**Doctor** (2)**Dr.** Newell's history course; she is majoring in (3)**social science** (4)**Social Science.**   21. ____ ____

22. Jim moved to eastern Arizona; (1)**He** (2)**he** bought over (3)**400** (4)**four hundred** acres of land.   22. ____ ____

23. She knows (1)**four** (2)**4** students who are going to (3)**College** (4)**college** this fall.   23. ____ ____

24. Many (1)**hispanic** (2)**Hispanic** students have immigrated to this (3)**country** (4)**Country** because of political turmoil in their homeland.   24. ____ ____

67. SPELLING: RECOGNIZING CORRECT FORMS

(Study 70-73, Spelling)

Write the number of the **correctly spelled** word.

Example: A knowledge of (1)**grammar** (2)**grammer** is helpful. ___1___

1. (1)**Athletics** (2)**Atheletics** can be both healthful and enjoyable. 1._____
2. Glenn hopes to add (1)**playright** (2)**playwright** to his list of professional credentials. 2._____
3. No one thought that a romance would (1)**develope** (2)**develop** between those two. 3._____
4. Mrs. Smith will not (1)**acknowlege** (2)**acknowledge** whether she received the check. 4._____
5. I love to (1)**surprise** (2)**surprize** the children with small presents. 5._____
6. The children were taught to be (1)**courtous** (2)**courteous** to adults. 6._____
7. One of the volunteers will be (1)**ninety** (2)**ninty** years old next week. 7._____
8. The salary will depend on how (1)**competant** (2)**competent** the employee is. 8._____
9. I loved listening to Grandpa's tales about his childhood because he always (1)**exagerated** (2)**exaggerated** the details. 9._____
10. It's important to accept valid (1)**criticism** (2)**critcism** without taking the comments personally. 10._____
11. He offered several (1)**ridiculous** (2)**rediculous** excuses for his behavior. 11._____
12. (1)**Approximately** (2)**Approximatly** fifty families attended the adoption support group meeting. 12._____
13. The murder was a (1)**tradegy** (2)**tragedy** felt by the entire community. 13._____
14. I could not remember the definition of (1)**nucleus** (2)**nuclious**. 14._____
15. Everyone could hear the (1)**argument** (2)**arguement** between the two young lovers. 15._____
16. Tim asked several questions because he wasn't sure what the professor (1)**ment** (2)**meant** by a "term paper of reasonable length." 16._____
17. The professor was offended by the (1)**ommission** (2)**omission** of his research data. 17._____
18. Carrying a portable telephone seems a (1)**necessary** (2)**neccessary** precaution. 18._____
19. Every time I visit Aunt Nan, she likes to (1)**reminisce** (2)**reminice** about her youth. 19._____
20. Meeting with a tutor for an hour before the examination was a (1)**desperate** (2)**desparate** attempt by Tom to pass his math class. 20._____
21. Susan was excited about her (1)**nineth-** (2)**ninth-**grade graduation ceremony. 21._____
22. Sally needed a lot of (1)**repetition** (2)**repitition** in order to memorize the formulas for her next chemistry test. 22._____
23. How (1)**definite** (2)**defenite** is their decision to return to Texas? 23._____

24. The weight loss program offered a (1)**guarantee** (2)**garantee** that I would lose at least ten pounds. 24. _____

25. Jake hoped his temporary job would become a (1)**permenent** (2)**permanent** position. 25. _____

26. I always bring back a (1)**souvenir** (2)**suvinir** for my children when I travel on business. 26. _____

27. We were glad that the (1)**auxilary** (2)**auxiliary** lights came on during the severe thunderstorm. 27. _____

28. Rodney, unfortunately, had not (1)**fulfilled** (2)**fullfilled** the requirements for graduation. 28. _____

29. In our state, students in the (1)**twelth** (2)**twelfth** grade must pass a basic skills test. 29. _____

30. This year, our five-year-old son began to question the (1)**existance** (2)**existence** of the tooth fairy. 30. _____

31. When Loretta turned (1)**forty** (2)**fourty**, her office mates filled her office with black balloons and threw her a surprise party. 31. _____

32. Alex said that one of the worst aspects of life in Russia was the government's (1)**suppression** (2)**suppresion** of religious activity. 32. _____

33. Jack (1)**use to** (2)**used to** run a mile five times a week. 33. _____

34. Unfortunately, I find chocolate—any chocolate—(1)**irresistable** (2)**irresistible**. 34. _____

35. All three of my children are heading towards (1)**adolescence** (2)**adolesence**. 35. _____

36. The (1)**phychologist** (2)**psychologist** arranged a group program for procrastinators. 36. _____

37. My mother's suggestion actually seemed quite (1)**sensible** (2)**sensable**. 37. _____

38. The (1)**Sophomore** (2)**Sophmore** Class voted to sponsor a dance next month. 38. _____

39. An (1)**erroneous** (2)**erronous** announcement appeared in the local newspaper. 39. _____

40. The high school's star athlete was a (1)**conscientous** (2)**conscientious** student. 40. _____

41. The (1)**rythm** (2)**rhythm** of the song was perfect for our skating routine. 41. _____

42. My friend decided to (1)**persue** (2)**pursue** a degree in sociology. 42. _____

43. I don't have time for (1)**questionaires** (2)**questionnaires**. 43. _____

44. Robert's (1)**perseverance** (2)**perserverence** led to his ultimate success in the theater. 44. _____

45. She has a (1)**tendancy** (2)**tendency** to do her best work early in the day. 45. _____

46. Her services had become (1)**indispensible** (2)**indispensable** to the firm. 46. _____

47. A reception was held for students having an (1)**excellent** (2)**excellant** scholastic record. 47. _____

48. Joan saved her (1)**mathamatics** (2)**mathematics** course for her senior year. 48. _____

49. You will find no (1)**prejudice** (2)**predjudice** in our organization. 49. _____

50. Caldwell is (1)**suposed** to (2)**supposed** to deliver the lumber some time today. 50. _____

68. SPELLING: CORRECTING ERRORS

(Study 70-73, Spelling)

Write **1** if the word is spelled **correctly**.
Write **0** if it is spelled **incorrectly**; then write the correct spelling.

Example: hindrance	1 _____	
Example: vacum	0 vacuum	
1. unusualy	1. ___ _____	
2. oppinion	2. ___ _____	
3. criticize	3. ___ _____	
4. familar	4. ___ _____	
5. proceedure	5. ___ _____	
6. artical	6. ___ _____	
7. pursue	7. ___ _____	
8. accross	8. ___ _____	
9. confident	9. ___ _____	
10. maneuver	10. ___ _____	
11. relieve	11. ___ _____	
12. absense	12. ___ _____	
13. sacrefice	13. ___ _____	
14. mischievious	14. ___ _____	
15. prevalent	15. ___ _____	
16. parallel	16. ___ _____	
17. noticeable	17. ___ _____	
18. disasterous	18. ___ _____	
19. indepindent	19. ___ _____	
20. bussiness	20. ___ _____	
21. acquire	21. ___ _____	
22. truely	22. ___ _____	
23. government	23. ___ _____	
24. apologize	24. ___ _____	

25. controlling	25. ___ _____
26. sincereley	26. ___ _____
27. safty	27. ___ _____
28. synonim	28. ___ _____
29. catagory	29. ___ _____
30. imaginery	30. ___ _____
31. managment	31. ___ _____
32. amateur	32. ___ _____
33. reguler	33. ___ _____
34. hygiene	34. ___ _____
35. cemetery	35. ___ _____
36. preform	36. ___ _____
37. bookkeeper	37. ___ _____
38. monkeys	38. ___ _____
39. persistant	39. ___ _____
40. curiosity	40. ___ _____
41. stimulent	41. ___ _____
42. villian	42. ___ _____
43. knowledge	43. ___ _____
44. optimism	44. ___ _____
45. embarass	45. ___ _____
46. eighth	46. ___ _____
47. maintenence	47. ___ _____
48. entailing	48. ___ _____
49. happyness	49. ___ _____
50. doesn't	50. ___ _____

69. SPELLING: CORRECTING ERRORS

(Study 70-73, Spelling)

Write the number of the **misspelled** word; then write the misspelled word **correctly.**

	Column 1	Column 2	Column 3	Column Number	Correct Spelling
Example:	definate	opinion	already	1	definite
1.	prevalent	guarantee	preserverence	1._____	_____
2.	forty	discription	procedure	2._____	_____
3.	criticism	tradegy	fulfill	3._____	_____
4.	exagerate	suppression	used to	4._____	_____
5.	acquired	pursue	auxilary	5._____	_____
6.	acknowledge	truely	unusually	6._____	_____
7.	apparant	maneuver	parallel	7._____	_____
8.	ryhthm	restaurant	psychology	8._____	_____
9.	sensible	dosn't	maintenance	9._____	_____
10.	personaly	ninth	twelfth	10._____	_____
11.	argument	curiousity	secretary	11._____	_____
12.	sensable	erroneous	meant	12._____	_____
13.	schedule	dialogue	questionaire	13._____	_____
14.	nucleus	sacrefice	mischievous	14._____	_____
15.	accross	playwright	perform	15._____	_____
16.	guidance	ommission	independent	16._____	_____
17.	fasinating	opportunity	reminisce	17._____	_____
18.	hindrance	develop	hypocricy	18._____	_____
19.	catagory	acquaintance	management	19._____	_____
20.	existance	eighth	courteous	20._____	_____
21.	synonym	mathamatics	particularly	21._____	_____
22.	vacuum	suvenir	supposed to	22._____	_____
23.	definite	neccessary	repetition	23._____	_____
24.	permanant	condemn	business	24._____	_____
25.	meant	surprize	sophomore	25._____	_____
26.	analisis	criticize	excellent	26._____	_____
27.	prejudise	persistent	adolescence	27._____	_____
28.	irrelevent	conscientious	approximately	28._____	_____
29.	irresistible	knowlege	height	29._____	_____
30.	article	sacrifise	ridiculous	30._____	_____
31.	permissable	calendar	apologize	31._____	_____
32.	schedule	sincerly	absence	32._____	_____
33.	commitee	desperate	discipline	33._____	_____

70. SPELLING : WORDS FREQUENTLY MISSPELLED

(Study 70-73, Spelling)

Write the **letter missing** in the word.
Write **0** if no letter is missing.

Example: gramm r   _a_

1.	suppr ssion	1._____	21.	math matics	21._____
2.	tend ncy	2._____	22.	pre judice	22._____
3.	adol scence	3._____	23.	par llel	23._____
4.	nucl us	4._____	24.	erron ous	24._____
5.	defin te	5._____	25.	prev lent	25._____
6.	permiss ble	6._____	26.	rest urant	26._____
7.	perm nent	7._____	27.	rep tition	27._____
8.	guid nce	8._____	28.	nec ssary	28._____
9.	d scription	9._____	29.	sacr fice	29._____
10.	fascinat ing	10._____	30.	compet nt	30._____
11.	gu rantee	11._____	31.	questionna re	31._____
12.	abs nce	12._____	32.	tru ly	32._____
13.	appar nt	13._____	33.	exist nce	33._____
14.	hindr nce	14._____	34.	excell nt	34._____
15.	crit cism	15._____	35.	sch dule	35._____
16.	develop	16._____	36.	independ nt	36._____
17.	indispens ble	17._____	37.	irresist ble	37._____
18.	am teur	18._____	38.	consc entious	38._____
19.	argu ment	19._____	39.	opp ortunity	39._____
20.	me nt	20._____	40.	acknowl dge	40._____

Write **1** if the missing letters are **ie**.
Write **2** if the missing letters are **ei**.

1.	h__r	1._____	6.	v__n	6.____
2.	ach__ve	2._____	7.	ch__f	7.____
3.	dec__ve	3._____	8.	l__sure	8.____
4.	c__ling	4._____	9.	th__r	9.____
5.	w__rd	5._____	10.	w__gh	10.____

71. USAGE: WORDS SIMILAR IN SOUND

(Study 80, The Right Word)

Write the number of the **correct** choice. Answers should be based on formal usage and nonsexist language.

Example: (1)**Your** (2)**You're** lovelier than ever. _____2_____

1. Take my (1)**advice** (2)**advise**, Julius; stay home today. 1._____

2. The contract was (1)**alright** (2)**all right** until one of the partners began to steal from the company. 2._____

3. If you (1)**break** (2)**brake** the car gently, you won't feel a jolt. 3._____

4. Camping trailers with (1)**canvas** (2)**canvass** tops are cooler than hardtop trailers. 4._____

5. The diamond tiara stolen from the museum exhibit weighed more than three (1)**carets** (2)**carats**. 5._____

6. The Dean of Students Affairs doubted whether the young man was a (1)**credible** (2)**creditable** witness to the fight in the dining hall. 6._____

7. Over the (1)**course** (2)**coarse** of the next month, the committee will review the sexual harassment policy. 7._____

8. Helping Allie with history was quite a (1)**decent** (2)**descent** gesture, don't you agree? 8._____

9. This little (1)**device** (2)**devise** will revolutionize the personal computer industry. 9._____

10. The professor made an (1)**allusion** (2)**illusion** to a recent disaster in New York City when describing crowd behavior. 10._____

11. The (1)**children** (2)**kids** in my class are interested in learning about science. 11._____

12. She was one of the most (1)**eminent** (2)**imminent** educators of the decade. 12._____

13. We knew that enemy troops would try to (1)**envelop** (2)**envelope** us. 13._____

14. The lawyer wasn't (1)**enthused** (2)**enthusiastic** about her new case. 14._____

15. Go (1)**fourth** (2)**forth**, graduates, and be happy as well as successful. 15._____

16. Despite their obvious differences, the five students in Suite 401 had developed a real friendship (1)**among** (2)**between** themselves. 16._____

17. The software game created by Frank really was (1)**ingenious** (2)**ingenuous**. 17._____

18. The supervisor (1)**should of** (2)**should have** rewritten the memo. 18._____

19. She tried vainly to (1)**lessen** (2)**lesson** the tension in the house. 19._____

20. The van needed a new battery (1)**besides** (2)**plus** an oil change. 20._____

21. The style of furniture is actually a matter of (1)**personal** (2)**personnel** taste. 21._____

22. Even though Gary studied hard and attended every class, he discovered that he was (1)**disinterested** (2)**uninterested** in majoring in chemistry. 22._____

23. The judge (1)**respectfully** (2)**respectively** called for the bailiff to read the jury's questions. 23._____

24. When the grand marshal gave the signal, the parade (1)**preceded** (2)**proceeded.**

24. _____

25. Middle-aged professionals are forsaking their high-powered life-styles for a (1)**quiet** (2)**quite** existence in the country.

25. _____

26. (1)**Weather** (2)**Whether** to pay off all her creditors was a big question to be resolved.

26. _____

27. We were so overweight that we bought a (1)**stationary** (2)**stationery** bicycle for our fifth anniversary.

27. _____

28. The laser printer produces a much sharper image (1)**than** (2)**then** the older dot-matrix printer.

28. _____

29. The computer operator read (1)**thorough** (2)**through** most of the manual before finding a possible solution.

29. _____

30. The ability to pass doctoral qualifying exams is essentially a (1)**rite** (2)**right** of passage.

30. _____

31. She is the first (1)**woman** (2)**women** to umpire in this league.

31. _____

32. (1)**Your** (2)**You're** aware, aren't you, that the play is sold out?

32. _____

33. This scanner will (1)**complement** (2)**compliment** your computer.

33. _____

72. USAGE: WORDS SIMILAR IN SOUND

(Study 80, The Right Word)

Write the number of the **correct** choice. Answers should be based on formal usage and nonsexist language.

Example: William is (1)**to** (2)**too** (3)**two** clever for his own good.   _____2_____

1.   The agreement was (1)**among** (2)**between** Harvey and me.   1._____

2.   I wanted to go to the party, (1)**but** (2)**but yet** I had to study.   2._____

3.   The student was (1)**anxious** (2)**eager** to receive his award at the banquet.   3._____

4.   These graphs (1)**complement** (2)**compliment** your written work perfectly.   4._____

5.   "Go (1)**forth** (2)**fourth** to see those popcorn balls!" shouted the Boy Scout leader.   5._____

6.   The best advice is to take a long walk if you (1)**lose** (2)**loose** your temper.   6._____

7.   I'd rather be right (1)**than** (2)**then** President!   7._____

8.   Knowing that they have sufficient funds will (1)**lessen** (2)**lesson** their financial worries.   8._____

9.   The salesperson wrote a memo (1)**in regards to** (2)**regarding** the drastic change in sales.   9._____

10.   Some of the television producers were (1)**censored** (2)**censured** because they were showing violent programs before 9 p.m.   10._____

11.   Nobody (1)**accept** (2)**except** Gloria would stoop so low.   11._____

12.   Sam unplugged his phone, locked his door, and worked (1)**continuously** (2)**continually** on his research paper.   12._____

13.   His remark revealed his (1)**ingenious** (2)**ingenuous** nature because he never locked his car, no matter where he parked it.   13._____

14.   Her approach for preparing for the history final was (1)**different from** (2)**different than** my strategy.   14._____

15.   (1)**Everyone** (2)**Every one** of the computers was destroyed by the flood.   15._____

16.   If John (1)**passed** (2)**past** the physics final, it must have been easy.   16._____

17.   George Bush (1)**preceded** (2)**proceeded** Bill Clinton as President.   17._____

18.   The library copy of the magazine had lost (1)**its** (2)**it's** cover.   18._____

19.   For (1)**instance**, (2)**instants**, this computer doesn't have enough memory to run that particular word processing package.   19._____

20.   The firm is (1)**already** (2)**all ready** for any negative publicity from the outcome of the law suit.   20._____

21.   Can you name the (1)**capitals** (2)**capitols** of all fifty states?   21._____

22.   The committee, unfortunately, may have misunderstood (1)**your** (2)**you're** intentions.   22._____

23.   His physical condition showed the (1)**affects** (2)**effects** of inadequate rest and diet.   23._____

24. (1)**Irregardless** (2)**Regardless** of the weather, I plan to drive to Florida for the weekend.

24. _____

25. The country was (1)**quiet** (2)**quite** displeased by the diplomat's insensitivity to cultural differences.

25. _____

26. The steep (1)**descent** (2)**decent** down the mountain road was hazardous.

26. _____

27. Shall we dress (1)**formally** (2)**formerly** for the Senior Ball?

27. _____

28. To be an effective teacher had become her (1)**principal** (2)**principle** concern.

28. _____

29. Are you certain that the bracelet is made of ten-(1)**carat** (2)**carrot** gold?

29. _____

30. The Farkle family were (1)**altogether** (2)**all together** in the living room when the grandmother announced that she was willing her money to a nearby cat sanctuary.

30. _____

31. The student (1)**inferred** (2)**implied** from the professor that the final exam would be challenging.

31. _____

32. If Sam (1)**had** (2)**would** have attended class more often, he would have passed the first examination.

32. _____

33. "I, (1)**to** (2)**too** (3)**two**, have a statement to make," she said.

33. _____

34. Homelessness—(1)**its** (2)**it's** no longer just an American problem.

34. _____

35. Chris feels (1)**good** (2)**well** about the results of the faculty survey.

35. _____

36. He said, "(1)**Their** (2)**There** (3)**They're** is no reason for you to wait."

36. _____

37. The writer (1)**inferred** (2)**implied** that most Americans know little of international politics.

37. _____

38. "(1)**Whose** (2)**Who's** there?" she whispered.

38. _____

39. The cat ran behind my car, and I accidentally ran over (1)**its** (2)**it's** tail.

39. _____

40. The consultant will (1)**ensure** (2)**insure** that the audit is completed on time.

40. _____

41. Many employees feel that their decision to smoke at home is a (1)**personal** (2)**personnel** choice to make and not the company's to make.

41. _____

42. The twins (1)**formally** (2)**formerly** attended a private college in California.

42. _____

43. The mere (1)**cite** (2)**site** (3)**sight** of Julia made his heart soar.

43. _____

44. The new car had a (1)**device** (2)**devise** to register the outside temperature.

44. _____

45. (1)**Hopefully** (2)**We hope** that the instructor will post our grades before we leave for the holidays.

45. _____

46. The rap artist defended the lyrics of his latest album by discussing the (1)**principal** (2)**principle** of personal empowerment.

46. _____

47. The comic's act was vulgar and his manners (1)**coarse** (2)**course**.

47. _____

48. If Americans realized that secondary smoke causes thousands of lung-cancer deaths yearly, (1)**than** (2)**then** perhaps fewer parents would smoke at home.

48. _____

49. Will people be standing in the (1)**aisles** (2)**isles** at the dedication ceremony?

49. _____

50. Dr. Smith is (1)**famous** (2)**notorious** for her educational research.

50. _____

51. "Sad movies always (1)**affect** (2)**effect** me that way," lamented Kay.

51. _____

52. This winter may decide (1)**weather** (2)**whether** the Communist Party regains control of Russia.

52. _____

53. The president suggested a (1)**canvas** (2)**canvass** of the members of the organization.

53. _____

54. He was obviously (1)**effected** (2)**affected** by the quiet beauty of his surroundings.

54. _____

55. Even after several proofreadings, the new (1)**stationary** (2)**stationery** had several errors in the address.

55. _____

56. The mayor presented the proposal (1)**himself** (2)**hisself**.

56. _____

57. The (1)**thorough** (2)**through** commission report indicated that approximately forty percent of American schools don't have enough textbooks in their classrooms.

57. _____

58. Jonathon had the (1)**presence** (2)**presents** of mind to make a sharp right turn and to step on the accelerator.

58. _____

59. The students are apathetic towards the football team and homecoming activities. (1)**That** (2)**This** problem will be addressed by the University Student Government.

59. _____

60. This biology textbook has a (1)**most unique** (2)**unique** front cover design.

60. _____

61. The principal expected the students' behavior to (1)**correspond to** (2)**correspond with** the school district's expectations.

61. _____

62. Dr. McBride is a distinguished and (1)**eminent** (2)**imminent** member of the faculty.

62. _____

63. The family has (1)**born** (2)**borne** the noise and dust of the nearby highway construction for several months.

63. _____

64. The teacher has reported the matter to the (1)**principal** (2)**principle**.

64. _____

65. (1)**Their** (2)**They're** leasing a truck because they can't afford the down payment to purchase a new one.

65. _____

66. The time capsule (1)**may be** (2)**maybe** the best way for the general public to understand how people lived one hundred years ago.

66. _____

67. Some (1)**individual** (2)**person** dropped off a package at the mailroom.

67. _____

68. The track coach told me that he wanted to (1)**discuss** (2)**discus** my performance at the last meet.

68. _____

69. The voters are (1)**apt** (2)**likely** to vote for a candidate who promises to reduce unemployment.

69. _____

70. "What is (1)**your** (2)**you're** candid opinion?" she asked.

70. _____

71. (1)**Who's** (2)**Whose** theory do you believe regarding the geographical origin of humankind?

71. _____

72. In the mountains we quickly felt the (1)**affects** (2)**effects** of a change in elevation.

72. _____

73. Jack used (1)**these kind of tools** (2)**this kind of tool** to repair the roof.

73. _____

74. Even with sophisticated computer analysis, the anthropologists weren't (1)**quiet** (2)**quite** sure of the origin and age of the skull.

74. _____

75. The (1)**council** (2)**counsel** (3)**consul** met to decide the fate of the student who cheated on the psychology final.

75. _____

73. USAGE

(Study 80, The Right Word)

Write in the number of the **correct** choice.

_____

Example: Willa wanted the doll very (1)**much** (2)**badly**.   ___1___

1.   Your essay has (1)**its** (2)**it's** faults, but it makes excellent points too.   1._____

2.   A tall tree has fallen and is (1)**laying** (2)**lying** across the highway.   2._____

3.   A significant (1)**percent** (2)**percentage** of Americans still smoke.   3._____

4.   In *The Oxbow Incident*, the wrong man is (1)**hung** (2)**hanged**.   4._____

5.   Did you ask if he will (1)**let** (2)**leave** you open a charge account?   5._____

6.   The new dance had (1)**to** (2)**too** (3)**two** many steps to remember.   6._____

7.   The student discovered that her backpack had (1)**burst** (2)**bursted** (3)**busted** because she was carrying too many books.   7._____

8.   We were disappointed (1)**somewhat** (2)**some** at the poor quality of the color printer.   8._____

9.   Sarah promised to (1)**learn** (2)**teach** me some gardening techniques.   9._____

10. Will the new legislation (1)**affect** (2)**effect** your business enterprise?   10._____

11. The Minority Scholars Program (1)**accepted** (2)**excepted** the resignation of the program director.   11._____

12. We were (1)**real** (2)**very** pleased that they came to the rodeo.   12._____

13. The computer operator (1)**waited for** (2)**waited on** a response over the Internet.   13._____

14. We heard the same report (1)**everywhere** (2)**everywheres** we traveled.   14._____

15. The tourists were not sure that it would be (1)**alright** (2)**all right** to travel to Great Britain this summer.   15._____

16. That the people are sovereign is the first (1)**principal** (2)**principle** of a democratic society.   16._____

17. As soon as he had (1)**affected** (2)**effected** his release, he telephoned her.   17._____

18. Do (1)**try to** (2)**try and** spend the night with us when you are in town.   18._____

19. The diplomat was (1)**most** (2)**almost** at the end of her patience.   19._____

20. Shooting innocent bystanders is one of the most (1)**amoral** (2)**immoral** street crimes committed.   20._____

21. The alfalfa milkshake may taste unpleasant, but it is (1)**healthy** (2)**healthful**.   21._____

22. The tennis player always (1)**lays** (2)**lies** down before an important match.   22._____

23. Timothy (1)**lay** (2)**laid** new linoleum on the floor of the recreation hall.   23._____

24. Unfortunately Tim is often (1)**compared to** (2)**compared with** his older brother.   24._____

25. It's a (1)**fact** (2)**true fact** that this type of van does not do well on safety tests. 25. _____

26. The (1)**amount** (2)**number** of trees needed to produce a single book should humble any author. 26. _____

27. The park officials were (1)**altogether** (2)**all together** satisfied with the new single-rail roller coaster. 27. _____

28. Over the past twenty years, we have witnessed several (1)**phenomena** (2)**phenomenon** out in the forest late at night. 28. _____

29. I (1)**had ought** (2)**ought** to have let her know the time of my arrival. 29. _____

30. They had (1)**already** (2)**all ready** canceled their reservations. 30. _____

31. The newspaper was soggy because it had (1)**laid** (2)**lain** in a rain puddle all morning. 31. _____

32. After spending $1,000 on repairs, we hope that the van finally works (1)**like** (2)**as** it should. 32. _____

33. The couple (1)**adapted** (2)**adopted** a baby girl from Bulgaria. 33. _____

34. Will you be sure to (1)**contact** (2)**get in touch with** me tomorrow? 34. _____

35. He (1)**seldom ever** (2)**hardly ever** writes to his sister. 35. _____

36. Cindy was (1)**besides** (2)**beside** herself with anger. 36. _____

37. The agreement was (1)**among** (2)**between** Harry and me. 37. _____

38. Do not (1)**set** (2)**sit** the floppy disk on top of the computer monitor. 38. _____

39. The play was from (1)**classical** (2)**classic** Rome. 39. _____

40. One reason for his poor health is (1)**because** (2)**that** he doesn't get enough sleep. 40. _____

41. The curtain was about to (1)**raise** (2)**rise** on the last act of the senior play. 41. _____

42. I wanted to go to Mary's party, (1)**but** (2)**but yet** I had to study. 42. _____

43. The customer was (1)**sure** (2)**surely** upset when she discovered that the warranty did not cover the repair. 43. _____

44. The (1)**children** (2)**kids** in my class are interested in the field trip. 44. _____

45. The camp is just a few miles (1)**farther** (2)**further** along the trail. 45. _____

46. I wrote to the registrar (1)**in regard to** (2)**in regards to** my missing transcript. 46. _____

47. The lawyer wasn't (1)**enthused** (2)**enthusiastic** about her new case. 47. _____

48. The news report (1)**convinced** (2)**persuaded** me to join a volunteer organization that renovates homes in low-income neighborhoods. 48. _____

49. The supervisor (1)**should of** (2)**should have** rewritten the memo. 49. _____

50. The van needed a new battery (1)**besides** (2) **plus** an oil change. 50. _____

74. USAGE

(Study 80, The Right Word)

Write **1** if the boldface expression is **correct**.
Write **0** if it is **incorrect**. (Formal, nonsexist usage is intended.)

Example: The car's fender was dented and **it's** windshield was cracked.   _0_

1. **Those sort** of books are expensive.   1._____

2. The cabin was **like** I remembered it from childhood vacations.   2._____

3. Some children look **like** their parents.   3._____

4. I was surprised that the banquet was attended by **lots of** people.   4._____

5. You **hadn't ought** to sneak into the show.   5._____

6. **It's** time for class.   6._____

7. You **too** can afford such a car.   7._____

8. We were **plenty** surprised by the outcome of our survey.   8._____

9. I **can't hardly** hear the speaker.   9._____

10. He studied **alot** for the biology lab exam.   10._____

11. Randy promised me that he is **over with** being angry with me.   11._____

12. **Irregardless** of the result, you did your best.   12._____

13. Will he **raise** your salary?   13._____

14. Try to keep him **off of** the pier.   14._____

15. I **always** stop at this corner meat market when I am having dinner guests.   15._____

16. Her **presence** is always intimidating.   16._____

17. His efforts at improving communication **among** all fifty staff members will determine his own success.   17._____

18. Her success was **due to** hard work and persistence.   18._____

19. I'm invited, **aren't I**?   19._____

20. **Their** house is now for sale.   20._____

21. Henry and **myself** decided to start a small business together.   21._____

22. The club lost **its** president.   22._____

23. Susan is **awfully** depressed.   23._____

24. Did he **lay** awake last night?   24._____

25. The professor's opinion **differed with** the teaching assistant's perspective.   25._____

26. Bob **laid** the carpet in the hallway.   26._____

27. I **sure** am sore from my exercise class.   27._____

28. He **better** get here before noon.   28._____

29. She is a **real** hard worker.   29._____

30. The cat **has been laying** on top of the refrigerator all morning.   30._____

31. I admire **that kind** of initiative.   31._____

32. He was **plenty** worried about the loan.   32._____

33. He has **plenty** of opportunities for earning money.   33._____

34. San Francisco offers many **things** for tourists to do.   34._____

35. **Most all** her friends are married.   35._____

36. The damage was **nowhere near** as severe as it was originally estimated to be.   36._____

37. He always did **good** in English courses.   37._____

38. The low price of the printer **plus** the modem prompted me to buy both.   38._____

39. **Because** her supervisor seemed unreasonable, Sue finally decided to resign.　　39.____

40. Max has **less** enemies than Sam.　　40.____

41. The speaker **inferred** that time management depended more on attitude than skill.　　41.____

42. Glenn has a long **way** to travel each week.　　42.____

43. Did he **loose** his wallet and credit cards?　　43.____

44. She looked **like** she was afraid.　　44.____

45. Walking to school was a **rite** of passage in our home.　　45.____

46. Who were the **principals** in the company?　　46.____

47. His finances are in bad **shape**.　　47.____

48. Have you written **in regards to** an appointment?　　48.____

49. Elaine **adopted** her novel for television.　　49.____

50. Damp weather **affects** her sinuses.　　50.____

75. USAGE

(Study 80, The Right Word)

Write the number of the **correct** choice.

Example: Fix it (1)**anyways** (2)**any way** you can.   ___2___

1. The author of that particular book was (1)**censored** (2)**censured** for his views
    by a national parenting group.   1._____

2. You may borrow (1)**any one** (2)**anyone** of my books if you promise to return it.   2._____

3. Compared (1)**to** (2)**with** the Steelers, the Raiders have a weaker defense but a
    stronger offense.   3._____

4. The figure of Venus de Milo is an excellent example of (1)**classic** (2)**classical**
    sculpture.   4._____

5. He (1)**should of** (2)**should have** notified his hostess of his change in plans.   5._____

6. The linebacking unit was (1)**composed** (2)**comprised** of Taylor, Marshall, and Burt.   6._____

7. Be (1)**sure to** (2)**sure and** review your class notes before the exam.   7._____

8. The young researchers considered everything (1)**accept** (2)**except** the truthfulness
    of their subjects.   8._____

9. (1)**Irregardless** (2)**Regardless** of difficulties, he will complete the project.   9._____

10. We (1)**better** (2)**had better** go over our presentation one more time.   10._____

11. The author was (1)**enthused** (2)**enthusiastic** about her next book topic.   11._____

12. The three children tried to outrun (1)**each other** (2)**one another**.   12._____

13. An early morning rainstorm has (1)**raised** (2)**risen** the level of the lake.   13._____

14. Near my hometown are several (1)**historic** (2)**historical** sites dating back to the
    Revolutionary War.   14._____

15. I spoke to the agent about (1)**ensuring** (2)**insuring** the cottage.   15._____

16. I am a neat person, (1)**aren't I** (2)**am I not** ?   16._____

17. Bagels were brought to this country by Jewish (1)**emigrants** (2)**immigrants** in the
    early 1900s.   17._____

18. My sociology book was (1)**setting** (2)**sitting** in the study carrel, where I had left it. 18._____

19. The speaker was (1)**real** (2)**really** dynamic.   19._____

20. Bob and (1)**I** (2)**myself** were glad that we saw the Comet Hyakutake last spring.   20._____

21. The actual (1)**percent** (2)**percentage** of commuters was a surprise to most
    administrators at our institution.   21._____

22. We had (1)**fewer** (2)**less** problems that we anticipated.   22._____

23. Dr. Brown, one of the most popular professors on campus, has a (1)**nice**
    (2)**pleasant** personality.   23._____

24. Don spent the day (1)**laying** (2)**lying** in the shade of our oak tree in the backyard. 24. _____

25. My sons always claim that any (1)**lose** (2)**loose** change in the couches and chairs is theirs to keep. 25. _____

26. The background music (1)**complemented** (2)**complimented** the poet's reading of her work. 26. _____

27. Dr. Baker's love for her students and the teaching process literally (1)**envelops** (2)**envelopes** all who enter her classroom. 27. _____

28. The house showed the obvious (1)**affects** (2)**effects** of long-term neglect. 28. _____

29. The deep-breathing exercises before the exam helped to (1)**lessen** (2)**lesson** Tony's test anxiety. 29. _____

30. The new policy will (1)**affect** (2)**effect** student contributions to their financial aid package. 30. _____

31. The award ceremony was (1)**preceded** (2)**proceeded** by a brief musical concert. 31. _____

32. Her former boyfriend walked (1)**past** (2)**passed** her without speaking. 32. _____

33. Stay for (1)**a while** (2)**awhile** before going to the library. 33. _____

34. A cloud of smoke was (1)**raising** (2)**rising** from the distant hillside. 34. _____

35. Will it be (1)**all right** (2)**alright** to spend more time on this project? 35. _____

36. After six consecutive losses, the debate team's (1)**moral** (2)**morale** is sagging. 36. _____

37. The leader's efforts to find the lost scouts was (1)**altogether** (2)**all together** praiseworthy. 37. _____

38. His peers considered him to be a man of high (1)**principals** (2)**principles**. 38. _____

39. Her attitude towards the problem was quite different (1)**from** (2)**than** his. 39. _____

40. The department (1)**used** (2)**utilized** a new graphics package to create the brochure. 40. _____

41. The newest employee receives (1)**less** (2)**fewer** assignments than the others working in the department. 41. _____

42. (1)**You're** (2)**Your** not going to believe what happened to me today! 42. _____

43. Stan told me that in his vocabulary there was (1)**no such a** (2)**no such** word as can't. 43. _____

44. Harriet told me an (1)**incredible** (2)**incredulous** story. 44. _____

45. Bridget planned the (1)**conference** (2)**conferrence** activity. 45. _____

46. The expense (1)**and** (2)**plus** the controversy surrounding the theme of their float prompted the one particular fraternity to cancel their participation in the homecoming parade. 46. _____

47. Rob worked for several weeks to (1)**device** (2)**devise** an attractive advertising campaign for the campus elections. 47. _____

48. A cloud of smoke was (1)**rising** (2)**raising** from the distant hillside. 48. _____

49. The politician (1)**to** (2)**too** was in agreement with the student activist's remarks. 49. _____

50. Kim (1)**counseled** (2)**counciled** Joan on how to set up an effective time management program. 50. _____

76. USAGE

(Study 80, The Right Word; and 81, Nonsexist Usage)

Write **1** if the boldface expression is **correct**.
Write **0** if it is **incorrect**. (Formal nonsexist usage is intended.)

Example: The day was **like** a bad dream.　　　1

1. A lion hunting its prey is **immoral**.　　1.____

2. The troop was **already** to leave for camp.　　2.____

3. The **men** and **girls** on the team played well.　　3.____

4. We split the bill **between** the three of us.　　4.____

5. **Almost** all of my friends came to my graduation party.　　5.____

6. The hum of the air conditioner was **continual**.　　6.____

7. The informer was **hanged**.　　7.____

8. The air conditioner runs **good** now.　　8.____

9. The child is **too** young to understand.　　9.____

10. **Irregardless** of his shortcomings, she loves him.　　10.____

11. Where is the party **at**?　　11.____

12. Please **bring** these plans to the meeting tomorrow.　　12.____

13. The **salesman** was looking forward to the sale.　　13.____

14. The sun will **hopefully** shine today.　　14.____

15. **Their** political strategy failed in the end.　　15.____

16. The **workmen** complained that the work site was unsafe.　　16.____

17. His chances for a promotion looked **good**.　　17.____

18. The twins frequently wear **one another's** clothing.　　18.____

19. A twisted branch was **laying** across our path.　　19.____

20. She was **disinterested** in the boring play.　　20.____

21. Send a cover letter to the **chair** of the department.　　21.____

22. The auditorium holds **less** than six hundred people.　　22.____

23. The hostile countries finally **effected** a compromise.　　23.____

24. The professor was somewhat annoyed at the **girls** in his class.　　24.____

25. Sam **differs from** Gina about the issue of increasing social services.　　25.____

26. I meant to **lay** down for just an hour.　26.____

27. Let's think **further** about it.　　27.____

28. **Hopefully** the weather will improve.　28.____

29. He enjoys the **healthy** food we serve.　29.____

30. Paul's **delusions** kept him from being employable.　　30.____

31. The **husband** and **wife** were both pursuing law degrees.　　31.____

32. Her position in the company was **most unique.**　　32.____

33. He has **already** departed.　　33.____

34. I will have to **rite** a letter to that company.　　34.____

35. **There's** was an informal agreement.　35.____

36. **Due to** the pollution levels, the city banned incinerators.　　36.____

37. Durnell is a student **which** always puts his studies first.　　37.____

179

38. John **respectfully** bowed when he was introduced to the Japanese dignitaries.   38.____

39. Tim was **mad** with love for her.   39.____

40. Only the **chairman** knew the exact amount in the budget.   40.____

41. She was **terribly** pleased at winning the content.   41.____

42. **Their** is always another game.   42.____

43. The gold locket had **lain** on the floor of the attic for ten years.   43.____

44. Our computer is older **then** your system.   44.____

45. Foyt **lead** the race from start to finish.   45.____

46. By his tone, the news reporter **implied** that the politician was guilty of fraud.   46.____

47. **Lie** down for a while.   47.____

48. The cost of living keeps **rising**.   48.____

49. **They're** writing a play together.   49.____

50. To find the missing watch, we ventured **further** into the crowd.   50.____

77. USAGE

(Study 80, The Right Word; and 81, Nonsexist Usage)

Write **1** if the boldface expression is **correct**.
Write **0** if it is **incorrect**. (Formal nonsexist usage is intended.)

Example: Nikki **sure** could sew.   0

1. Two of the rebels were **hanged.**   1.____
2. The **woman** doctor was quite supportive of her nursing staff.   2.____
3. Anne was happy **due to** her promotion.   3.____
4. Jamie **emigrated** from Mexico in 1988.   4.____
5. The phone rang **continually.**   5.____
6. The committee decided that the institution needed more **manpower** during registration.   6.____
7. The archeological dig reached the lowest **strata.**   7.____
8. His reasons are different **than** mine.   8.____
9. **On the basis of the report,** John was promoted.   9.____
10. Robert always wears attractive, **classical** business suits.   10.____
11. He wrote essays, short stories, **etc.**   11.____
12. June has **less** days than July.   12.____
13. Be **sure and** check the map before you leave.   13.____
14. He hiked **farther** than I.   14.____
15. Swimming is **healthful** exercise.   15.____
16. They **seldom ever** clean the office coffee pot.   16.____
17. There was a **bunch** of people in the waiting room.   17.____
18. The **aisles** in the new store were too narrow.   18.____
19. I **set** my packages on the table.   19.____

20. We need to find a reliable **repairman** to fix the air conditioner.   20.____
21. How about staying here for **awhile.**   21.____
22. I shall **contact** my attorney.   22.____
23. Roberto and Imaru were **anxious** to marry.   23.____
24. He fell **off** the ladder.   24.____
25. I am **nowhere near** ready to go.   25.____
26. Sue's balloon had **bursted.**   26.____
27. The temple **sits** on a high hill.   27.____
28. John **usually always** complained about his work schedule.   28.____
29. I asked in **regards** to my check.   29.____
30. What did the **individual** look like who stole the library book?   30.____
31. **Mankind** needs to seek peaceful solutions to international conflict.   31.____
32. The **brakes** on the bicycle need repairing.   32.____
33. The **reason** the stock prices increased is **because** the company had a good year.   33.____
34. The blanket was too **coarse** to use on a bed.   34.____
35. The cat has been **lying** on the hearth all afternoon.   35.____
36. I am sure that he will be **O.K.**   36.____
37. The supervisor **persuaded** her unhappy employee to take a brief leave of absence.   37.____
38. Audrey wrote a **fine** paper.   38.____

39. She does **well** in examinations.   39.____

40. The uniform looked **good** on her.   40.____

41. The psychiatrist was convinced that the defendant was **mad**.   41.____

42. The students created a mock exam **theirselves**.   42.____

43. Dillinger was a **notable** public enemy.   43.____

44. The reporter **laid** his notebook on the table.   44.____

45. The audience was **all together** bored by the second act of the play.   45.____

46. No modern playwright can be **compared to** Shakespeare.   46.____

47. All roads lead there. Take **anyone**.   47.____

48. When offered a pay cut or early retirement, most executives chose the **latter**.   48.____

49. The local community college will **except** you on a probationary status.   49.____

50. Is this test **verbal** or written?   50.____

78. USAGE

(Study 80, The Right Word; and 81, Nonsexist Usage)

Write **1** if the sentence is **correct**.
Write **0** if it is **incorrect**; then correct the error.
(Formal, nonsexist usage is intended.)

Example: Its been a unique experience.   <u> 0 </u>   <u> it's </u>

1. Some people drive their cars like everyone else on the road were a sworn enemy.   1. __ _____

2. The interview committee was altogether surprised by the candidate's response.   2. __ _____

3. The waitress snarled when I left a quarter for a tip.   3. __ _____

4. We wanted to lay in the sun for a week and forget about bosses, meetings, memos, and deadlines.   4. __ _____

5. Being jolted by fifty volts had little apparent affect on Harold, who insisted it had brightened his day.   5. __ _____

6. The comet was suppose to be visible on clear nights.   6. __ _____

7. Where is the cite for your web page?   7. __ _____

8. Irregardless of my grades, I'm an excellent writer, except for word usage.   8. __ _____

9. Please contact me when you arrive.   9. __ _____

10. After the hurricane, the neighborhood roads were in poor condition.   10. __ _____

11. I sometimes pace around my room when I'm trying to understand a complex thing.   11. __ _____

12. We were far too credible about the investment, and that's how we lost our capital.   12. __ _____

13. He better get to class on time because Professor Morrison does not like his class to be disturbed.   13. __ _____

14. How much farther do we need to travel?   14. __ _____

15. You're absolutely right to go to traffic court and dispute the ticket.   15. __ _____

16. Hopefully, the committee will meet soon to decide the scholarship awards.   16. __ _____

17. The number of deaths by gunshot wounds in the United States is incredulous.   17. __ _____

18. The explosion in the chemistry lab caused quite a commotion among the five lab assistants, who were working on their projects.   18. __ _____

19. The police officer which saved the little girl's life will receive a humanitarian award from the mayor's office.   19. __ _____

20. The antivirus software is far more effective than any of the other packages.   20. __ _____

79. NONSEXIST USAGE

(Study 80, The Right Word; and 81, Nonsexist Usage)

Write **1** if the sentence is **correct**.
Write **0** if it is **incorrect**; then correct the error.
(Formal, nonsexist usage is intended.)

Example: The woman scientist is messy around the office.   <u>0</u> The scientist

1.   The male and girl students decided to form separate groups.   1. __ _____

2.   Until the baby was three, I worried about my mothering skills.   2. __ _____

3.   Medical students now spend a portion of their class time discussing
     interpersonal communication strategies.   3. __ _____

4.   Every student must bring his textbook to class.   4. __ _____

5.   The policeman stationed in the parking garage will walk students to their cars.   5. __ _____

6.   In our neighborhood, the fathers staying home to raise their children organized a
     baby-sitting cooperative.   6. __ _____

7.   Man's need to survive produces some surprising effects.   7. __ _____

8.   Skaters competing in tournaments often spend five hours a day practicing
     their routines.   8. __ _____

9.   Girls, it is time that our spouses assume more responsibility for raising
     our children!   9. __ _____

10. The stewardess assured us that we would land in time for our connecting flight.   10. __ _____

11. A female cement-truck driver delivered the cement for our new driveway.   11. __ _____

12. The innkeeper, his wife, and his children greeted us when we arrived at the inn.   12. __ _____

13. The repairman's estimate was much lower than we had expected.   13. __ _____

14. Everyone hoped that his or her proposal would be accepted.   14. __ _____

15. When on an elevator, most people prefer riding in silence.   15. __ _____

16. The spinster who lives on our street never attends the block parties.   16. __ _____

17. The male nursing student in the post-surgery ward answered all of my questions.   17. __ _____

18. Because of gender, the male nursing student was a minority in his nursing class,
     because all of his classmates were women.   18. __ _____

19. The lady mathematics professor has published several textbooks.   19. __ _____

20. Mr. Feather's widow is searching for a job outside of the home.   20. __ _____

80. BEYOND THE SENTENCE: PARAGRAPH DEVELOPMENT WITH SPECIFICS

(Study 91, Effective Paragraphs)

<u>Underline</u> the **topic sentence** in each paragraph. In addition, write **1** if the paragraph develops its topic sentence adequately **and** then write another sentence that would continue its development. Write **0** if the paragraph is not adequately developed **and** then write the reason you think so.

1.   Today's athletes are overpaid. Although it is undeniable that not everyone can toss a basketball through a hoop or throw a baseball ninety miles an hour, that does not mean that fans should have to pay the admission prices they do. People who like sports have other ways to spend their money, such as on movies, vacations and hobbies. Many fans cannot even afford to go to sporting events. Doctors and nurses also perform valuable services to society; should they be rich enough to retire at thirty-five? The cost of living for the average person continues to climb. Athletes should not be millionaires, no matter how good they are at their particular sports.

1.   _____   _____
        _____
        _____

2.   School boards often eliminate extracurricular activities and athletic programs when they are faced with a budgetary crisis. However, such cutbacks are really detrimental to the well-being of their students, who are already feeling the pressure of life in the 1990s. Often students must cope with violence in their schools. Some students never know when someone will be seriously injured or killed in their schools or neighborhoods. Many students must resist the daily temptation of drugs and alcohol. Despite substance abuse programs in their schools and communities, teenagers remain targets for drug pushers who have infiltrated the playgrounds and classrooms. For some students, home life is no better. Dual-income and single-parent families force teenagers to fend for themselves after school—no milk and cookies and Mom waiting for these students. Educators should look for ways to reduce stress in the lives of their high school students. Extracurricular activities and sports programs help students achieve some sort of balance in their lives.

2.   _____   _____
        _____
        _____

3.   Baseball has given American English many expressions over the past 150 years. For instance, from the 1880s, baseball generated the following terms: *goose egg, double play, bunt, bullpen, shutout, bleachers, rain check, and doubleheader.* The origin of the term *bleachers* is unknown; however, some writers credit a Chicago sportswriter who said that fans sitting in an uncovered portion of a grandstand were "bleached" by the sun. Of course, baseball still gives us new vocabulary. Since the 1950s, we have learned to call sports enthusiasts *fans* or *cranks* because they supposedly crank up the home team with their cheering. Players who are chasing after practice fly balls are said to be *shagging* the balls, and those player engaged in a heated argument are described as having a *rhubarb*. These examples represent only a small sampling of the baseball vocabulary that has quietly slipped into our language.

3.   _____   _____
        _____
        _____

Multicutural curricula should provide opportunities for all students to explore their own cultures and the cultures of their classmates and communities. Frequently, schools focus on one or two cultures for classroom and assembly activities. Students from a European-American background may feel that they don't have a specific culture to share with their classmates; they may not know a second language, or have special cultural attire, food, or music. Their families' traditions may have been lost over the years or blended with America's commercialization of holidays. Multicultural activities should help every child, including those with European-American roots, to research not only special ceremonies but also everyday expressions of their culture.

4. _____ _____
   _____
   _____

5. At the beginning of the twentieth century, Americans needed better roads for their automobiles, and yet local, state, and federal governments were not interested in allocating funds to pay for new roads. In 1912, Carl Graham Fisher, founder of the Indianapolis 500 Speedway, proposed that Americans come together to donate funds for its first coast-to-coast highway. Fisher estimated that it would take $10 million in donations to construct a two-lane gravel road from New York City to San Francisco. By 1915, Fisher had enough donations to begin the highway, which he had decided to call the Lincoln Highway. Fisher felt that this name sounded patriotic; however, the name alienated many Southerners. Fisher worried about how to collect the rest of the money needed to complete the highway. Then he struck upon a unique fund-raising idea. Fisher constructed what he called "seedling miles"; that is, he paved dirt roads between towns in a number of locations along the route for the Lincoln Highway. As Fisher predicted, once people in these towns realized the benefits of paved road, they enthusiastically raised additional funds to extend the highway beyond their town borders. In 1923, the Lincoln Highway, which was the world's first transcontinental highway, officially opened, and it continued to be used for the next forty years.

5. _____ _____
   _____
   _____

81. BEYOND THE SENTENCE: PARAGRAPH UNITY

(Study 91, Effective Paragraphs)

<u>Underline</u> the **topic sentence** of each paragraph. Then, in the blank at the end of the paragraph, write the number(s) of any sentence(s) in the paragraph that **do not relate directly** to the topic sentence.

1.   (1)From a pebble on the shore to a boulder on a mountainside, any rock you see began as something else and was made a rock by the earth itself. (2)Igneous rock began as lava that over hundreds of years hardened far beneath the earth's surface. (3)Granite is an igneous rock that is very hard and used for buildings and monuments. (4)Sedimentary rock was once sand, mud, or clay that settled to the bottom of a body of water and was packed down in layers under the ocean floor. (5)All rocks are made up of one or more minerals. (6)Metamorphic rock began as either igneous rock or sedimentary rock whose properties were changed by millions of years of exposure to the heat, pressure, and movement below the earth's crust.

1.   _____   _____

2.   (1)Although we normally associate suits of armor with the knights of medieval Europe, the idea of such protective coverings is much older and more pervasive than that. (2)Some knights even outfitted their horses with metal armor. (3)As long as 3,500 years ago, Assyrian and Babylonian warriors sewed pieces of metal to their leather tunics the better to repel enemy arrows. (4)A thousand years later, the Greeks wore metal helmets, in addition to large metal sheets over their chests and backs. (5)Native Americans of the Northwest wore both carved wooden helmets and chest armor made from wood and leather. (6)Nature protects the turtle and the armadillo with permanent armor. (7)Even with body armor largely absent from the modern soldier's uniform, the helmet still remains as a reminder of the vulnerability of the human body.

2.   _____   _____

3.   (1)Mention the name of George Washington and most Americans envision a larger-than-life hero, who, even as a little boy, could not tell a lie. (2)However, it turns out that Washington was more human than his biographers would have us believe. (3)His contemporaries described Washington as moody and remote. (4)He was also a bit vain, for he insisted that his fellow officers address him as "Your Excellency." (5)He refused to allow himself to be touched by strangers. (6)Washington was also known to weep in public, especially when the Patriots' war effort was sagging. (7)Washington was even plagued with traitors, who gave the British advice on how to beat the Americans. (8)He was not even a gifted military officer. (9)Rather than a hero of the French and Indian War, Washington may have provoked the French to go to war by leading an unnecessary and irrational attack against a group of Frenchmen. (10)While Washington was certainly a brave man, dedicated to freeing the colonists from British tyranny, he was not the perfect man that early biographers described.

3.   _____   _____

4.   (1)In the mid-1800s, an apple or a pear was considered too dangerous to eat. (2)In fact, any fresh vegetable or fruit was considered too risky because one bite might lead to cholera, dysentery, or typhoid. (3)During cholera epidemics, city councils often banned the sale of fruits and vegetables. (4) The only safe vegetable was a boiled potato. (5)A typical breakfast might include black tea, scrambled eggs, fresh spring shad, wild pigeons, pig's feet, and oysters. (6)Milk was also considered a perilous beverage because many people died from drinking spoiled milk. (7)Milk was really a threat to people's health

because it was processed and delivered to home with little regard for hygiene. (8)Children and those who were ill were often malnourished because the foods with the most nutrients were also the most deadly. (9)Until the invention of the icebox in the 1840s, rich and poor people alike risked their health and even their lives every time they ate a meal.

4. _____ _____

82. BEYOND THE SENTENCE: PARAGRAPH COHERENCE—TRANSITIONS

(Study 91, Effective Paragraphs)

For each item, choose from the list the **transitional expression** that fits most logically in the space. Then write the number of that expression (**1** to **10**). There could be more than one correct answer.

1. **Afterward**   6. **Meanwhile**
2. **Consequently**   7. **Nevertheless**
3. **Even so**   8. **On the other hand**
4. **Formerly**   9. **That is**
5. **However**   10. **Therefore**

Example: I think. _____, I am.   ___10___

1. The night of the ball, we danced every step we knew. _____, we strolled on the moonlit beach.   1._____

2. By the late 1870s, Britons were looking forward to their weekend leisure time; _____, until the early 1890s, Americans were working sixty-hour, six-day weeks.   2._____

3. Money, _____ was not standardized in the United States until the Civil War when the federal government produced its first paper money.   3._____

4. Life in postwar America was secure and promising; _____, Americans were enjoying a strong economy, which provided plenty of jobs and high wages.   4._____

5. The term teenager entered the language only as recently as 1941; _____, teenagers were not really a recognized presence in American society.   5._____

6. When we speak to family members, we use an informal and intimate language. When we are speaking to a large group, _____, we are more likely to choose different words and a different tone of voice.   6._____

7. If you toss a coin repeatedly and it comes up heads each time, common sense tells you to expect tails to turn up soon. _____, the chances of heads coming up remain the same for each toss of the coin.   7._____

8. The first real movie—_____, one that actually had a story line—was the film entitled *The Great Train Robbery.*   8._____

9. American children spend about a quarter of their waking time watching television; _____, it is important to monitor what young children are watching.   9._____

10. A seven-hundred pound microwave oven, called the Radarange, was first produced by Tappan in 1955. _____, Americans were not interested in purchasing a microwave oven until the late 1960s when the appliance was much smaller and more reliable.   10._____

83. BEYOND THE SENTENCE: BIBLIOGRAPHIC FORM

(Open-Book Exercise—Study 93, The Reference List)

Write **1** if the entire entry is **correct** in form.
Write **0** if the entry contains any error in form (including punctuation).
Circle the error. For Part I of this exercise, use the **MLA** style.

1.	Book	Bamberger, Jeanne S., and Howard Brofsky. <u>The Art of Listening: Developing Musical Perception</u>. 2nd ed. New York: Harper, 1972.	1. _____
2.	Book	Blanche Ellsworth, and John A. Higgins. <u>English Simplified</u>. 8th ed. New York: Longman, 1997.	2. _____
3.	Book	Boorsten, Daniel J. The Creators: <u>A History of Heroes of the Imagination</u>. Random House: New York, 1992.	3. _____
4.	Journal Article	Hirsch, Glenn. <u>Helping Students Overcome the Effects of Difficult Learning Histories</u>. "Journal of Developmental Education" 18.2 (1994): 10-12, 14.	4. _____
5.	Newspaper Article	Heider, Timothy. "Stadium Panel Calls for Using Same Site." <u>The Plain Dealer</u> 20 April 1996: A1.	5. _____
6.	Encyclopedia Article	Lewis, Ronald L. "Frederick Douglass." <u>The 1996 Grolier Multimedia Encylopedia</u>. 1996.	6. _____
7.	Magazine Article	Novak, Michael. "A Call for Disunity." <u>Forbes</u> 9 July 1990:65.	7. _____
8.	CD-ROM	"Oregon Trail II: An Interactive Virtual Trail Adventure." CD-ROM. Minneapolis: The MECC Learning Library, 1994.	8. _____
9.	Article in a Collection	Reed, Ismael; "America: The Multinational Society." <u>Multicultural Journey Through Reading and Writing</u>. Ed. Marilyn Smith Layton. New York: Harper, 1991.	9. _____
10.	Journal Article	Pintozzi, Frank. "Culture and Its Implications for Learning Among Second Language Students." <u>Journal of College Reading and Learning</u>. 26.2 (1995): 45-53.	10. _____

Write **1** if the entire entry is correct in form.
Write **0** if the entry contains any error in form (including punctuation).
Circle the error. For Part II of this exercise, use the **APA** style.

1.	Book	Kingsbury, P. (1995). <u>The Grand Ole Opry: History of country music.</u> New York: Villard Books.	1. _____
2.	Editor	Gonzalez, R (Editor.). (1992). <u>After Aztlan: Latino poets of the nineties.</u> Boston: David R. Godine.	2. _____

3.	**Newspaper Article**	Graeff, B. (1996, April 21). "Indians' defense kicks in." *The Plain Dealer*, p. D7.	3. _____
4.	**Book**	King P. M. and Kitchener K. S. (1994). <u>Developing reflective judgment: Understanding and promoting intellectual growth and critical thinking in adolescents and adults.</u> San Francisco:Jossey-Bass.	4. _____
5.	**Book**	Martin, D. (1991, 2nd ed.). *How to be a successful student.* San Anselmo, California: Martin Press.	5. _____
6.	**Book**	Rose, M. (1995). *Possible Lives:* The Promise of Public Education in America. New York: Houghton Mifflin.	6. _____
7.	**Magazine Article**	Walman, S. (1992, May 4). "Deadbeat dads." *Newsweek,* 46-49	7. _____
8.	**Article in Collection, Editor**	Wieder, D.L., & Pratt, S. (1990). On being a recognizable Indian among Indians. In D. Carbaugh (Ed.), Cultural Communication and intercultural contact. Hillsdale, N.J. Lawrence Erlbaum Associates, 1990.	_____ 8. _____
9.	**Book**	Burnham, P. (1995). How the other half lived: a people's guide to American historic sites. Boston: Faber and Faber.	9. _____
10.	**Book, Editor**	Rabil, A. (Ed.). (1988). *Renaissance humanism.* Philadelphia: University of Pennsylvania Press.	10. _____

84. DOCUMENTATION

(Open-Book Exercise—Study 92, Citations; and 94, Endnotes and Footnotes)

Write **1** for each item that is **correct** in form.
Write **0** for each that is **incorrect**, and circle the error.

Use the **MLA** style.

---

1. Text
Farb feels that language is needed to make sense of life's experiences.[1]

1. _____

2. Footnote
[1]Peter Farb, Word Play: What Happens When People Talk (New York:Random House, 1973).

2. _____

3. Text
Rose observes that "life in schools and classrooms is vulnerable to the disruptions in the communities around them." [2]

3. _____

4. Footnote
[2]Rose, Mike, Possible Lives: The Promise of Public Education in America (New York: Houghton Mifflin, 1995) 424.

4. _____

5. Text
Burnham observes that many of America's historic sites still portray events and groups of people from strictly a European-American male perspective [4].

5. _____

6. Footnote
[4]Philip Burnham. How the Other Half Lived: A People's Guide to American Historic Sites (Boston: Faber and Faber, 1995).

6. _____

7. Text
Daly advises that college students will respond more positively to courses stressing thinking skills rather than to the traditional developmental reading and writing courses. 10

7. _____

8. Footnote
[10] William T. Daly, "Thinking As an Unnatural Act", Journal of Developmental Education 18.2 (1994): 29.

8. _____

9. Footnote
(The paper cites two works by the same author.)
[17]Hennings, One Knowing 234.

9. _____

10. Footnote
(This writer is citing two or more works by Rose.)
[8]Rose, Possible 133.

10. _____

85. ACHIEVEMENT TEST: GRAMMAR

(Study 29, Effective Sentences: Avoid These Faullts in Sentence Construction)

Write **1** if the boldface expression is **one complete sentence**.
Write **2** if it is a **fragment**.
Write **3** if it is a **comma splice** or **fused sentence** (run-on).

Example: Having completely slipped its moorings. _____2_____

1. He decided not to go. **After buying the tickets and packing his bags.** 1._____

2. I have been working to reach two goals. **To lose thirty pounds and to get my adult children to leave home.** 2._____

3. **He will attend college, his high school grades are good enough.** 3._____

4. The rancher sold most of his livestock. **Then he turned his property into a profitable dude ranch.** 4._____

5. **Based on a recent study.** Over 69 percent of workers earning a minimum wage are twenty or older. 5._____

6. **When does abstract art become just scribbles?** 6._____

7. **Our guests having arrived, we sat down to dinner.** 7._____

8. Nine families joined the pollution study. They will wear carbon-filter badges, **this device will monitors the air that they are breathing.** 8._____

9. **The storm having washed out the bridge.** We had to spend the night in town. 9._____

10. Sir Thisby invited me to play cricket. **A game I had never even watched.** 10._____

11. **The high humidity forced us to move the picnic inside, it was just too hot to eat outside.** 11._____

12. **The student who tape-records the physics lecture.** 12._____

13. **I continued to watch the baseball game on television even though I had not started my calculus homework that was due the next day.** 13._____

14. **Allen used a week's vacation.** To sand and refinish the hardwood floors in his home. 14._____

15. **Aaron always told his family that he wanted to be a physician,** however, he secretly dreamed of running off to New York to study acting. 15._____

Write **1** if the boldface expression is used **correctly**.
Write **0** if it is used **incorrectly**.

Example: There **was** laughing, singing, and shouting coming from the dorm. _____0_____

1. Osnir and **myself** were responsible for the decorations at the Fiesta. 1._____

2. During the summer, she trained horses, **which** assisted her financially. 2._____

3. In this mall **are** a child-care facility, an adult literacy school, and a large discount store. 3._____

4. Cousin Max, along with his twin daughters and their cats, **were** waiting at my front door.   4. _____

5. The interviewer asked each of the politicians to explain **their** position on taxation.   5. _____

6. Copies of *Esquire* and *Rolling Stone* **was** in Dr. Moore's waiting room.   6. _____

7. The taxi driver gave Tony and **I** a scornful glance.   7. _____

8. The ticket agent gave Ed and **me** seats that were behind home plate.   8. _____

9. Every committee member **was** given a copy of the report.   9. _____

10. **Refusing to pay high interest**, consumers are cutting up their credit cards.   10. _____

11. Parking restrictions apply **not only** to students **but also** to visitors.   11. _____

12. His mother wanted him to become a corporate lawyer. **This** kept Leonard in college.   12. _____

13. Students should meet their professors, **so that if you have questions about class, you'll feel comfortable approaching a professor during office hours.**   13. _____

14. **Having an hour to kill,** there was time to stroll through the village.   14. _____

15. His plans included **landing a well-paying internship and to spend as much time as possible with his girlfriend.**   15. _____

16. **Being nervous about the speech**, the microphone amplified my quavering voice.   16. _____

17. We wondered why the list of courses **was** not posted yet.   17. _____

18. There are few people who write in a personal journal as much as **her**.   18. _____

19. I like **swimming** and **to relax** in the warm sunshine.   19. _____

20. Aggression **is when** one nation attacks another without provocation.   20. _____

21. **Is** either of the two bands ready to go on?   21. _____

22. **Who** wrote the editorial on campus racism in this week's school newspaper?   22. _____

23. Everyone who plays the lottery hopes that **their** ticket will the million-dollar jackpot.   23. _____

24. **Us** students refuse to pay more in tuition next quarter!   24. _____

25. All of **we** residents living in the Sussex area were upset when a fast-food restaurant was built nearby.   25. _____

26. Financial aid will be made available to **whoever** shows a need for it.   26. _____

27. Every student should understand that it is up to **you** to find the strategies to do well academically.   27. _____

28. He coached Little League and joined two service clubs. **It** was expected of him by his associates.   28. _____

29. Harry and **myself** solved the crime of the missing coffee pot in the lounge.   29. _____

30. **Who** do you think will apply for the position of Dean of Students?   30. _____

31. There **was** at least eight persons involved in the traffic accident.   31. _____

32. Between you and **I**, Martin has only a slim chance of promotion this year.   32. _____

33. **Is** there any objections to your opening a nightclub on campus?   33. _____

34. My advisor suggested that I take Russian. **That** was fine with me.   34. _____

35. Each of the players **has** two passes for all home games.   35. _____

36. Neither Joan nor her two attendants **was** asked to appear on television.   36. _____

37. He is one of the engineering students who **have** a summer internship.   37. _____

38. You will never find anyone more responsible than **her**.   38. _____

39. Jenette is the **friendliest of the two resident assistants in my building**.   39. _____

40. My personal **stationery** consists of a yellow legal pad and some white business envelopes.   40. _____

41. Why not give the keys to **whomever** you think will be in charge?   41. _____

42. Did the committee approve of **his** assuming the chair position?   42. _____

43. Several of **we** students had decided to start a petition addressed to the deans.   43. _____

44. In his backpack **were** a notebook computer, an umbrella, and his lunch; he was prepared for a day on campus.   44. _____

45. The coach, as well as the manager and players, **was** sure of winning.   45. _____

46. **Knowing of his parents' disapproval**, it seemed wise for him to reconsider his plan to drop out of school to become a skydiving instructor.   46. _____

47. Daniel decided to **only** purchase three new fish for his aquarium.   47. _____

48. If he **were** more tactful, he would have fewer enemies.   48. _____

49. The supper for the African American and Latino club officers was a success, **in fact,** most agreed that this event should be funded every semester.   49. _____

50. Neither the camp director nor the hikers **was** aware of their danger.   50. _____

51. He purchased the only book that **was** of any value to him for his senior project.   51. _____

52. The specialist's report suggested that my wife and **I** consider adoption.   52. _____

53. **Predicting the success of the new food service on campus.**   53. _____

54. The faculty **are** working together to develop a more culturally inclusive curriculum.   54. _____

55. Each of the students **plans** to attend the career fair.   55. _____

56. The poor writing and sloppiness of your research **forces** me to fail this essay.   56. _____

57. Did anyone lose **his** calculator last night in the computer center?   57. _____

58. *Watching the Birds* **is** the title of his latest play.   58. _____

59. When the Buffalo Bills and the Pittsburgh Steelers play, I know **they** will win.   59. _____

60. To everyone's surprise, the lottery winner announced that five hundred dollars **was** to be given to all of her immediate and distant relatives.   60. _____

86. ACHIEVEMENT TEST: PUNCTUATION

Write **1** if the punctuation in brackets is **correct**.
Write **0** if it is **incorrect**.
(Use only one number in each blank.)

Example: Stuart took lessons in using[,] word processing.

_0_

1. Salt Lake City, Utah[,] was their first stop on the trip east.

1._____

2. The neighbors[,] who own the barking dog[,] refuse to do anything about their noisy pet.

2._____

3. I wanted to call on the Madisons, but I wasn't sure which house was their['s].

3._____

4. Our flight having been announced[,] we hurried to board the plane.

4._____

5. We went for a ride in the country[.] The day being warm and balmy.

5._____

6. When I open [it's] favorite cat food, the cat races into the kitchen.

6._____

7. Haven't you often heard it said, "Haste makes waste["?]

7._____

8. Wouldn't you like to go to the rally with us?"[,] asked the girl across the hall.

8._____

9. He said, "Let's walk across the campus.["]["]It's such a warm evening."

9._____

10. Enrollment is up to three[-]thousand students this quarter.

10._____

11. Twenty[-]six students have volunteered to serve on various committees.

11._____

12. Dear Sir[;] I have enclosed my application and resume.

12._____

13. After you have finished your sociology assignment[,] let's go to a movie.

13._____

14. Billy Budd struck Claggart[,] because he could not express himself any other way.

14._____

15. You did agree to give the presentation[,] didn't you?

15._____

16. We were early[;] as a matter of fact, we were first among the guests to arrive. 16._____

17. "If you really look closely," the art critic commented[,] "you'll see a purple turtle in the middle of the painting."

17._____

18. Dr. Johnson had little praise for the current health care system[;] calling it an elitist structure.

18._____

19. The band recorded its first album in the spring[,] and followed it with a summer concert tour.

19._____

20. She had hoped to arrange a two month[']s tour of Korea and Japan. 20._____

21. We hope[,] Ms. Foster[,] that your office will be satisfactory.

21._____

22. The next stockholders' meeting is scheduled for August 9, 1997[,] but it will be open only to major investors. 22._____

23. All the cars[,] which were speeding[,] were stopped by the police.

23._____

24. Because she played cards until midnight[;] she overslept.

24._____

25. Jane Cox[,] a biochemistry major[,] won the top scholarship.

25._____

26. Professor Thomas was asked to create a course for the Women[']s Studies Department.

26._____

27. The little boy in the center of the old photograph[,] would later write five novels.

27._____

28. "As for who has written the winning essay[—]well, I haven't as yet heard from the judges," said Mr. Hawkins. 28._____

29. What he described about the massive oil spill [,] filled us with horror.

29._____

30. I asked Elizabeth what we should do about our vacation plans[?]   30._____

31. The newly elected officers are Denzell Jones, president[;] Ruby Pillsbury, vice president[;] and Maria Garcia, secretary.   31._____

32. Before the radical group surrendered[;] they attempted to negotiate their freedom.   32._____

33. We followed the trail over several ridges[,] and along the edge of two mountain lakes.   33._____

34. Before touring Europe, I had many matters to attend to[;] such as making reservations, buying clothes, and getting a passport.   34._____

35. Having a good sense of humor helps you put problems into perspective[;] certainly it's better than brooding.   35._____

36. The ticket agent inquired ["]if we were planning to stop in Paris.["]   36._____

37. Once retired, Ensel painted portraits of family pets[,] and played bingo every Thursday and Saturday.   37._____

38. Marcia learned that all foods[,] which are high in fat[,] should be eaten in moderation.   38._____

39. We were told to read ["]Ode to a Nightingale,["] a poem by Keats.   39._____

40. The alumni magazine had a column cleverly entitled ["]Grad-Tidings.["]   40._____

41. A civilian conservation corps could provide[:] education, training, and work for thousands of unemployed teenagers. 41._____

42. Some people wish to have ["]America, the Beautiful["] become our national anthem.   42._____

43. She hurried towards us[,] her books clasped under her arm[,] to tell us the good news.   43._____

44. The audience wanted him to sing one more song[;] however, he refused.   44._____

45. My children want a CD-ROM reference entitled ["]The Grolier Multimedia Encyclopedia["] to look up information for their school reports.   45._____

46. She found a note in her mailbox: "Sorry to have missed you. The Lawson[']s.   46._____

47. His mother wanted him to major in chemistry[;] he wanted to major in music.   47._____

48. Chris decided that he wanted a quiet vacation[,] not one full of schedules and guided tours.   48._____

49. He had gone to the library[. B]ecause he wanted to borrow some videos.   49._____

50. Her program included courses in English[,] social science[,] and chemistry.   50._____

51. The two women, not having very much in common[;] found very little to say to each other.   51._____

52. To prepare for the baseball tryouts[,] Sam practiced every night.   52._____

53. Ms. Whitney, who is a physical education instructor, came to the rally[;] with Mr. Martin, who is the football coach.   53._____

54. When the tornado hit eastern Ohio[,] it caused millions of dollars of damage.   54._____

55. "Some of the seniors wer[']ent able to pay their dues," she said.   55._____

56. Frank Anderson[,] who is on the tennis team[,] is an excellent athlete.   56._____

57. "All motorists[,] who fail to stop at the crosswalk[,] should be put in jail!" declared an angry parent.   57._____

58. Looking at me sweetly, Mark replied, "No[,] I will not lend you a thousand dollars."   58._____

59. George enrolled in a course in home economics; Elsa[,] in a course in woodworking.   59._____

60. "Haven't I met you somewhere before?"[,] he asked.   60._____

61. "It's most unlikely["!] she said, turning away.   61._____

62. A student[,] whom I had met at the banquet[,] would like to work in our department next semester.   62._____

63. New commuter train systems are inexpensive to develop[,] where tracks are already in place. 63._____

64. He moved to Denver[,] where he worked as a freelance photographer. 64._____

65. We were[,] on the other hand[,] not surprised by his decision. 65._____

66. I bought a special type of paintbrush to reach those hard[-]to[-]reach spots near the rain gutters. 66._____

67. Listen to the arguments of both speakers[,] then decide which side you favor. 67._____

68. At the beginning of the week[;] I made a list of everything I needed to complete. 68._____

69. Susannah is familiar with many customs of Sweden [(]her father's homeland[)] and can prepare many Swedish dishes. 69._____

70. Our ex[-]mayor pleaded guilty to a speeding ticket. 70._____

71. The conference sponsored by our fraternity was successful[,] especially the sessions concerning community-service projects. 71._____

72. The printer made[,] a squealing noise before it began spewing out sheets of paper. 72._____

73. Jack displayed a unique [(?)] talent when he created a collage of spaghetti sauce, pickles, and pancakes. 73._____

74. The children[,] on the other hand[,] were content to wear last year's coats and boots. 74._____

75. The teenager used the word [*like*] throughout her conversation. 75._____

87. ACHIEVEMENT TEST: MECHANICS, SPELLING, USAGE

Capitalization

Write **1** if the boldface word(s) **follow** the rules of capitalization.
Write **0** if they **do not**

Example: Uncle Spike is their **Shortstop**.		0
Example: Their shortstop is **Uncle Spike**.		1
1.	I barely passed **spanish**.	1. _____
2.	My brother attends **High School**.	2. _____
3.	She is **President** of her class.	3. _____
4.	I belong to a **Science Club**.	4. _____
5.	He plays for Ohio **State**.	5. _____
6.	We saluted the **american** flag.	6. _____
7.	My **Uncle** plays third base for a major league baseball team.	7. _____
8.	I asked **Grandmother** to loan me the family album.	8. _____
9.	He enjoys living in the **Southwest**.	9. _____
10.	The **Eastern** side of the house needs to be repainted.	10. _____
11.	Janet enjoys **History** 101.	11. _____
12.	I visited an **indian** village while on vacation.	12. _____
13.	Anna works full time and attends the **University**.	13. _____
14.	He naps in his **history** class.	14. _____
15.	Study; **Prepare** for the last test and the final.	15. _____
16.	"What," **he** asked, "are you doing in my kitchen at 4 a.m.?"	16. _____
17.	"What," Jack asked, "**Is** wrong with your cat?"	17. _____
18.	We met on **New Year's Eve**.	18. _____
19.	The note began, "My **Dear** John."	19. _____
20.	I am going to be a **Medical Anthropologist**.	20. _____

Abbreviations and Numbers

Write **1** if the boldface abbreviation or number is used **correctly**.
Write **0** if it is used **incorrectly**.

Example: 2's company; three's a crowd.	0

1. Today is her **20th** birthday.   1. _____

2. Thank God it's **Fri.**   2. _____

3. My cat named Holiday is **5.**   3. _____

4. We live on Sutherland **Rd.**   4. _____

5. She was born on July **6th**, 1980.   5. _____

6. Please meet me at **10 o'clock**.   6. _____

7. He released **two hundred** pigeons at the picnic.   7. _____

8. After a brief investigation, we discovered that **13** students were involved in the prank.   8. _____

9. The train leaves at **8** p.m.   9. _____

10. Dinner was served at **six o'clock**.   10. _____

11. Joan Allen, **Ph.D.,** spoke first.   11. _____

12. Lunch cost **12** dollars!   12. _____

13. **Ms**. Martin, please chair the meeting today.   13. _____

14. Lloyd's monthly salary is now **$3,200.50.**   14. _____

15. The May **Co.** had a fire at the University Heights location.   15. _____

Spelling

In each sentence, one boldface word is **misspelled**; write its number in the blank.

Example: (1)**Their**(2)**questionnaries** have been (3)**received**.   ___2___

1. (1)**It's** (2)**unusual** for him to be so (3)**conscientous**, isn't it?   1. _____

2. The open (1)**cemetary** gates permitted an (2)**excellent** (3)**opportunity** for Karloff's laboratory assistant.   2. _____

3. My (1)**psychology** (2)**proffessor** assigns a weekly (3)**written** report.   3. _____

4. He needed (1)**permission** from the (2)**commitee** to participate in the (3)**competition**.   4. _____

5. The (1)**first-year** student learned that a (2)**knowledge** of (3)**grammer** is helpful.   5. _____

6. A (1)**fourth** such disaster threatens the very (2)**existance** of the Alaskan (3)**environment**.   6. _____

7. Arthur (1)**definately** considered it a (2)**privilege** to help write the (3)**article**.   7. _____

8. The (1)**principal** (2)**complimented** her for her (3)**excellant** performance.   8. _____

9. It was (1)**apparent** that she was (2)**desparate** by her listening to his (3)**advice**.   9. _____

10. We (1)**imediately** became (2)**familiar** with the requirements for a (3)**license**.   10. _____

11. Is it (1)**permissable** to ask him to (2)**recommend** me for a (3)**government** position?   11. _____

12. (1)**Personaly**, I didn't believe his (2)**analysis** of the result of the (3)**questionnaire**. 12. _____

13. The test pilot felt enormous (1)**optimism** after her third (2)**repitition** of the dangerous (3)**maneuver**.   13. _____

14. It's (1)**ridiculus** that Sue became so angry about the (2)**criticism** of her friend, the (3)**playwright**.   14. _____

15. She was not (1)**conscious** of being (2)**unnecessarily** (3)**persistant** about the matter.

15._____

Usage

Write **1** if the boldface expression is used **correctly** and follows the rules for formal, nonsexist language. Write **0** if it is used **incorrectly**.

Example: **Irregardless** of what you say, I'm buying a new car.

    ___0___

1. I was not **altogether** amused.

1._____

2. Aaron looked **sort of** tired after the test.

2._____

3. They are all old; for **instants**, Grayson is eighty-six.

3._____

4. Billy cried when his balloon **burst**.

4._____

5. Next time plan to invite **fewer** guests.

5._____

6. He earned no interest on his **principal**.

6._____

7. **Can** I add your name as a contributor to the scholarship fund?

7._____

8. The judge would hear no **farther** arguments.

8._____

9. I am in real trouble, **aren't I**?

9._____

10. The team was **plenty** angry.

10._____

11. The parent **persuaded** her child to take out the garbage.

11._____

12. He notified **most** of his creditors.

12._____

13. She knows **less** people than I.

13._____

14. Saul made an **illusion** to *Hamlet*.

14._____

15. Was the murderer **hanged**?

15._____

16. Helen feels **some** happier now.

16._____

17. The **kids** were excited.

17._____

18. I had **already** signed the check.

18._____

19. John sounds **like** he needs a vacation.

19._____

20. I can't stand **those kind** of jokes.

20._____

21. He is **real** happy about winning the contest.

21._____

22. The cat is **lying** by the fire.

22._____

23. She **generally always** works hard.

23._____

24. He does **good** in math courses.

24._____

25. His speech **implied** that he would raise taxes.

25._____

88. ACHIEVEMENT TEST: DOCUMENTATION

(Open-Book Exercise—Study 92-94, Documentation)

Part I:MLA style.

Write **1** for each bibliographic entry that is **correct** in form.
Write **0** for each that is **incorrect** and circle the error.

1. **Book**   Kent, David. <u>Forty whacks: new evidence in the life and legend</u>
                      <u>of Lizzie Borden</u>. Emmaus, PA: Yankee Books, 1992.   1. _____

2. **Journal**
    Article   Mallon, Jeffrey V. "Reading Science." <u>Journal of Reading</u>
                      34 (1991): 324-338.   2. _____

3. **Newspaper**
    Article   Navarro, Nireya. <u>Ethics of Giving AIDS Advice Troubles Catholic</u>
                      <u>Hospitals</u>. "The New York Times" 3 January 1993: A1.   3. _____

Part II: APA Style

Write **1** for each bibliographic entry that is correct in form.
Write **0** for each that is incorrect, and circle the error.

1. **Book**   Cheney, Lynne V. (1995). Telling the Truth. New York: Simon & Schuster.   1. _____

2. **Magazine**
    Article   Samuelson, R.L. (1992, May 11). "The bored billionaire." <u>Newsweek,</u>
                      119(19), 72.   2. _____

3. **Journal**
    Article   Richgels, Donald J. (1995). Invented spelling ability and printed word
                      learning in kindergarten. *Reading Research Quarterly*, 30(1),
                      96-109.   3. _____

PART III: MLA Style

Write **1** for each citation that is **correct** in form.
Write **0** for each that is **incorrect**.

1. **Direct**
    Quotation   According to a recent study of college students, "23 percent
                      spent no time at all on required reading during their entire
                      college career." (Douglas 175)   1. _____

2. **Paraphrase**   Douglas observes that many of the new student activities on campus are not closely related to intellectual pursuits (172).

2. _____

PART IV: APA Style

Write **1** for each citation that is **correct** in form.
Write **0** for each that is **incorrect**.

---

1. **Paraphrase**   Osborne (1989) reports that competent children have parents who encourage their children to play independently.

1. _____

2. **Direct Quotation**   Osborne (1989) observes that the majority of television programs contain violence; in fact, studies reveal that there are "five violent acts per hour during prime time" (page 83).

2. _____

A LIST OF GRAMMATICAL TERMS

The following chart gives brief definitions, examples, and nonexamples of the grammatical terms you'll read about most often in these exercises. Refer to English Simplifled for more information.

Term	What It Is or Does	Examples	Nonexamples
Adjective	Describes a noun	a **fast** runner (describes the noun **runner**)	He runs **fast** (describes the verb **runs**)
Appositive	A noun that renames another	Tom Wolfe, **the writer**, lives in New York. (The appositive follows the man's name.)	**Tom Wolfe,** the writer, lives in New York.
Adverb	Describes a verb, adjective, or another adverb	He runs **fast** (describes the verb **run**) He runs **very** fast (describes the adverb **fast**) He is an **extremely** fast runner (describes the adjective **fast**)	He is a **fast** runner. (Here, **fast** is an adjective.)
Clause	A group of words with a subject and a predicate. A main clause can stand by itself and make complete sense; a dependent clause must be attached to a main clause.	**He is a fast runner.** (A main clause) **if he is a fast runner** (A dependent clause that must be attached to some main clause; for example, **He will win.**)	a **fast runner** (merely a noun and its adjective)
Complement	Completes the meaning of the verb.	<u>Direct Object:</u> He threw the **ball**. (Says what got thrown.) <u>Indirect Object:</u> He threw the ball to **me.** (Says who benefited by the bail being thrown.) <u>Subjective Complement:</u> He is a **pitcher.** (Renames the subject **He** after the linking verb **is.**) <u>Objective Complement:</u> The team named Rodgers **coach.** (Follows the direct object **Rodgers** and renames it.)	**He** threw the ball. (Says who did the action rather than received it.)
Conjunction	A word that joins.	<u>Coordinating conjunction:</u> Joins things of equal importance: Men **and** women. Poor **but** honest. <u>Subordinating Conjunction:</u> Joins a dependent clause to a main clause: I left **when** she arrived	I left **at** noon. (**At** is a preposition.)

Fragment	A group of words that cannot stand by themselves and make complete sense.	**when I saw them** (a dependent clause) **from Maine to California** (a prepositional phrase)	**They went from Maine to California.** (a main clause that can stand by itself)
Noun	Names a person, place, animal, or thing.	**Tom, Denver, cat, book**	**throw** (a verb) **red** (an adjective)
Phrase	A group of words without a subject and a verb.	**from California** (a prepositional phrase) **to see the king** (an infinitive phrase) **built of bricks** (a participial phrase) **building houses** (a gerund phrase)	**He is from California.** (a main clause)
Predicate	The part of the sentence that speaks about the subject.	The man **threw the ball.** (says what the subject did)	The **man** threw the ball. (The **man** performed the action.)
Pronoun	A word that replaces a noun.	**He** will be here soon. (**He** takes the place of the man's name.)	**Jonathan** will be here soon. (**Jonathan** is a noun.)
Subject	The person or thing about whom the sentence speaks.	**Polly** writes children's books.	Polly **writes children's books.** (**Writes children's books** is the predicate, that is, the action she performs.)
Verb	Says what the subject either does or is.	She **buys** seashells. She **is** smart.	**Emily** is smart. (**Emily** is a noun.)

TEACHING-LEARNING AID: DIAGRAMMING

Diagraming is a method of analyzing sentences and of visually depicting parts of speech and their functions in sentences. Though diagrams can grow complex, their basic principle is simple: Everything in the complete subject is written to the left of the main vertical line; everything in the complete predicate, to the right. All the main parts of a sentence are written on or above the main horizontal line; all the secondary parts, below the main horizontal line.

Simple sentence

An old friend from school often sends me very funny postcards.

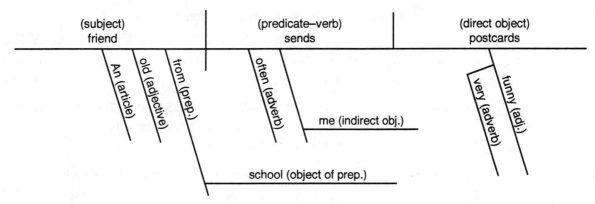

Simple sentence with compund parts

Romeo and Juliet fell in love and planned a secret wedding.

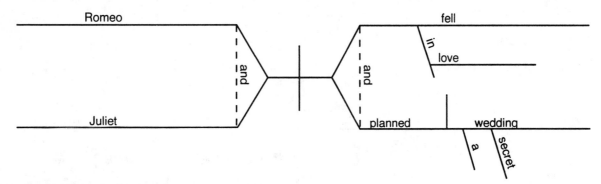

Verbals and verbal phrases
Used as modifiers

Reeling under our attacks (participial phrase), the *decimated* (participle) enemy requested a truce *to arrange a surrender* (infinitive phrase).

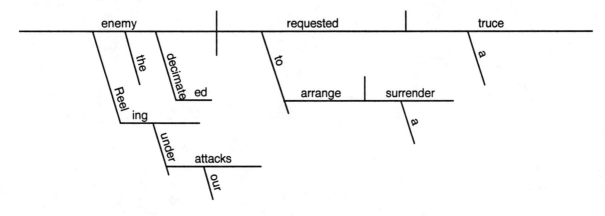

Verbals and verbal phrases
Used as nouns

They denied *having tried to embezzle funds by falsify-ing data.* (Italicized words are a gerund phrase: within that phrase are an infinitive phrase, *to embezzle funds,* and another gerund phrase, *falsifying data.*)

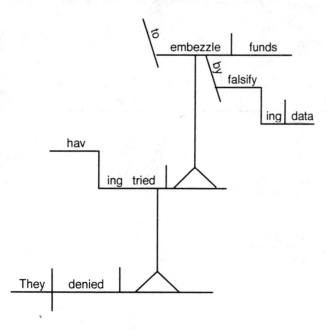

Compund sentence

We tried hard, but we failed badly.

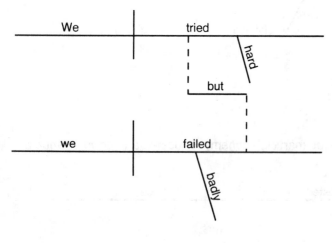

Complex sentence
With adjective clause (dotted line between relative pronoun and antecedent)

I respect a person *who can resist pressure.*

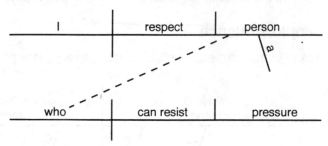

Complex sentence
With adverb clause (dotted line between verb of adverb clause and word the clause modifies)

We will continue our campaign *until we make Jones mayor.*

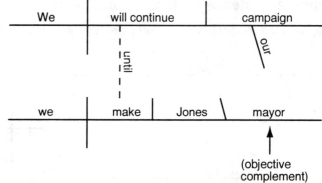

With noun clause (on tower)

You should take *whatever you can get.*

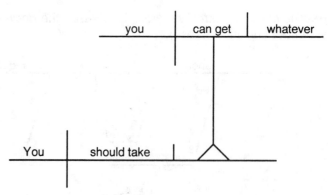

That you will succeed is almost certain.

Give it to *whoever answers the door.*

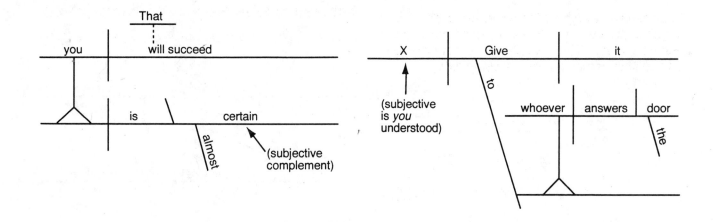